IMAGES
of England

AROUND
BURTON UPON TRENT
LOOKING BACK

Burton became a Municipal Borough from 3 September 1878 and then proudly embraced County Borough status from 1 April 1901 until 1 April 1974 when the town became part of the East Staffordshire District under local government reorganization. This multi-view postcard from around 1903 shows conventional town views but the scroll design is imaginative, incorporating ale casks, hops and barley.

IMAGES
of England

AROUND
BURTON UPON TRENT
LOOKING BACK

Compiled by
Geoffrey Sowerby and Richard Farman

TEMPUS

Tempus Publishing Limited
The Mill, Brimscombe Port,
Stroud, Gloucestershire, GL5 2QG

ISBN 0 7524 1596 4

Typesetting and origination by
Tempus Publishing Limited
Printed in Great Britain by
Midway Clark Printing, Wiltshire

A pleasant scene at Alrewas in the early 1920s. This village was to make national news on 15 May 1967 when a Burton gas fitter, George Taylor, was in Alrewas to convert the first house from town gas to natural gas in front of press and television cameras (several times in fact, to satisfy them all). Burton and district was chosen as the first area in the conversion programme, which involved adapting appliances in 13 million homes. 'C-Day' began in the villages of Alrewas and Fradley, and Burton was the first town to have its gas changed.

Contents

Men from Burton and district were quick to answer the call to the colours in the Boer War and a Half Service Company of Volunteers left for South Africa in March 1900. They were soon followed by a relief section and then by a second Half Service Company, who are photographed here before departure. The group are posed on the river bank near the cricket pavilion and rifle range on Bass's Meadow with the Wetmore skyline behind them. Back row, left to right: Privates F. Tuckey, C.D. Yeomans, E.F. Greenwood, G. Powis, J.H. Downs, A. Mason, E.V. Stevens, T.G. Stephenson, W.A. Johnson, J.W. Curtis. Middle row: Privates A.C. Ward, J.R. Jeffs, W. Satchwell. W. King, W.J. Sparrow, J. Bartram, W. Toon, A. Goodhead, W. Webster, G. Evans, W.F. Baker, C. Whieldon. Front row: Bugler F.W. Soloman, L/Cpl W. Burton, Cpl H.B. Hart, Sgt-Major G.A. Maher, Captain and Adjutant H.N. Head, Captain C.E. Boote, Sgt J.S. Pountney, Cpl E. Farrington, L/Cpl H.J. Wright, Private A. Gibbs (stretcher bearer). In 1900 the Volunteers of the 2nd Battalion, Prince of Wales' North Staffs. Regiment had their headquarters at Bass premises, 54/55 High Street. Lord Burton was the Honorary Colonel and the senior officers were R.F. Ratcliff and J. Gretton. In 1907 the Volunteers became part of the Territorial Force and the former Bell Hotel in Horninglow Street became the drill hall in 1912.

One
A Century of Memories

The year 1900 dawned with British troops fighting in South Africa, the Boer War having broken out in 1899. Initially, Britain suffered humiliating defeats which marred the early days of 1900. The commencement of the year seems to have been quite low-key everywhere, partly because of the Boer crisis but also due to very lively public disagreement about the starting date of the new century.

Heated controversy in the correspondence columns of The Times *finally gave way in February 1900 to the news of the relief of Ladysmith and then, in May, of Mafeking. These events were enthusiastically celebrated, creating an upsurge of optimism and pride, although the final Boer surrender did not come about until 31 May 1902.*

The fact remains that a large majority of the public thought that the last new century began in 1901 and they would have maintained that we are launching an enormous and expensive celebration after only ninety-nine years of the twentieth century.

Most Burtonians certainly seem to have regarded 1901 as the significant date. One man in no doubt at all was the redoubtable William Walters, Bass Traffic Manager and organizer of the famous Bass trips. Introducing his enlarged souvenir booklet for the 1901 Great Yarmouth visit, he reviewed the achievements of the previous 100 years and referred to 'Our first excursion handbook of the New Century.' Good attendance at watch-night services seems to have been the principal local commemoration along with midnight bells, whistles and hooters.

Soon, however, there were more momentous happenings, both nationally and locally. Queen Victoria's long reign ended with her death on 22 January 1901, followed by the Proclamation of King Edward VII and later by his Coronation. In the early days of the Edwardian era troops were excitedly welcomed home from South Africa and the king also visited Burton in 1902. These were the occasions that made the greatest impact on the town and townsfolk. They provide our starting point as we commence 'Looking Back' and recalling some of the events and memories of the old century.

Following Queen Victoria's death, the Prince of Wales was nationally declared King and on Saturday 26 January 1901, following tradition, he was formally proclaimed in Burton. National mourning made it a subdued occasion but crowds followed a procession of dignitaries to the Market Place. After a fanfare the Mayor, Councillor Morris, ordered 'hats off'. People stood bareheaded (a rare occurrence for this period) to hear the Proclamation. All verses of the National Anthem were sung and the mayor led three cheers for the King and three more for Alexandra, Queen Consort, to end the ceremony.

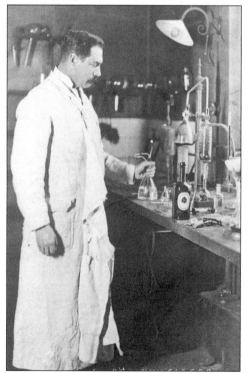

In 1902 King Edward VII was the guest of Lord Burton at Rangemore Hall and was enthusiastically welcomed throughout his drive through the town to visit the Bass brewery, where he started the special brew known as 'King's Ale'. This photograph of the Bass laboratory shows James O'Sullivan analysing this famous beer. James was the brother of Cornelius O'Sullivan and they were just two of many distinguished chemists who worked in the Burton brewing industry and who formed a society of professional chemists known as the Bacterium Club.

Between the 1860s and the early 1930s migrant workers from East Anglia were a feature of local life. Many agricultural labourers became unemployed during the winter and came to Burton for the malting season. A Suffolk newspaper misprint once said they were in Burton for the mating season! Many were from Suffolk but others were from Norfolk and all came to be known as 'Norkies'. Three of them pose here for a souvenir picture, complete with malt shovels, outside a Bass malthouse. In the early 1900s around 400 Norkies were employed.

Burton's tramway system officially opened on August Bank Holiday Monday in 1903, but the first car over the new lines was pulled by four dray horses from the station yard to the foot of Station Bridge, launched onto the track and then hauled to the depot. The first electrically powered tram left the depot at 4.00 a.m. on 24 July for a test trip, three councillors leaving their beds to travel. They were delayed at Bargates when the trolley pole was wrenched off. This view of High Street in tramway days looking towards Bargates includes Allsopp's Lager Brewery and a typical level crossing.

There was much local interest in flying after the Burton Aviation Meeting of 1910. Members of the Model Aero Club regarded their models as serious scientific experiments. When the Navy introduced seaplanes at the 1912 Naval Review, the local club followed suit with their experimental models, seen here on the canal at Shobnall. Early military flying was in the hands of the Royal Naval Air Service until the Royal Flying Corps was established in 1912 as a branch of the Army. The Royal Air Force was formed on 1 April 1918 with the amalgamation of the RNAS and the RFC.

THE ENTIRE PUBLISHING PROFITS of the first 10,000 Copies have been devoted to the Relief Fund.

NO. 172
WITH TONIC SOL-FA.
This Song may be Sung in Public without Fee or License except at Theatres or Music Halls.

THE SHIP THAT WILL NEVER RETURN

(The Loss of the "Titanic.")

SONG
AND
POEM

Written & Composed
by

F. V. ST. CLAIR.

LONDON
E. MARKS & SON.
125, Mare Street Hackney, N.E.
and 35 Rosoman Street, E.C.

Few disasters have ever made a greater impact on the public than the loss of the *Titanic* on 15 April 1912. For the first time Burton Opera House was permitted to open on a Sunday (24 April) for a sacred concert in aid of victims. Among the music copies of a former Opera House musician was this speedily produced song. No one hearing its sorrowful verses could have imagined how the story would not only be kept alive all century through books and films but that the ship itself would be visited and photographed, and relics recovered.

In 1914 Burtonians enjoyed many hot summer days. Bank Holiday Monday saw them in thousands attending three local shows in perfect weather. Although war clouds seemed to be threatening, few could have conceived that next day, 4 August, Britain would declare war and the world be changed forever. This scene outside the drill hall in Horninglow Street captures the new sense of uncertainty: men speculating, the women anxious. Burton's volunteer reservists were quickly mobilized and then, from here, successive groups of new local volunteers marched away behind a band. The reality was that 1,300 Burtonians never came back.

Early in the century Burton had its share of women actively seeking equal voting rights with men. Locally, they belonged to the National Union of Women's Suffrage, not the more militant 'Suffragettes'. There was also a mild opposition from the Anti-Women's Suffrage League. In 1914, however, the nation's women united and were soon replacing men and performing jobs and duties to aid the war effort, often where women had never previously been employed. This photograph shows three young women among many who took over brewing and malting tasks in the Burton breweries.

Shell cases and ammunition boxes dominate in this First World War photograph of the extensive Dixie sidings, replacing the beer barrels which would once have been the principal feature. There are vans and wagons from many of the old pre-grouping companies, including one which must have been a local rarity from the Hull and Barnsley Railway. Burton's situation and extensive rail links and sidings made it an ideal distribution centre for war materials – another sphere in which many women were employed – while shell cases were manufactured locally. Prominent is the Midland bonded warehouse at Derby Turn.

After the war the town was presented with tank No. 286 carrying the name *Burtonia*. It is not widely known that Baguley Cars were involved in early secret work on the testing of tanks prior to their first military use in 1917. Tank tracks and propulsion were tested at the firm's Shobnall factory and on the Sinai hills where the 'Bullock Creeping Grip Tractor' was the subject of experimental trials. The Holt design was finally chosen but this presentation at the town hall acknowledged Burton's various contributions to the war effort.

Between 1924 and 1926 Trent Bridge, then the town's only river crossing by road, was widened on the north side from thirty feet to fifty feet to ease growing traffic problems. There was additional widening at the Swan junction to improve access to Bearwood Hill. This interesting photograph shows an arch of the ancient original Burton bridge, from the twelfth century or earlier, which was newly unearthed in 1924 during the early stages of excavations at the Winshill end of the bridge.

A Marston's brewery lorry dressed for a parade. The theme of the display is truly patriotic. Britannia, John Bull, Scotland, Wales and Ireland all appear with a collection of products, seemingly locally inspired, and messages such as 'Wake Up England – British Goods Are Still The Best' and 'British Engineers Are The Finest In The World'. Tyres, rubber, coal and farming are certainly represented. Costumes and the lorry's solid tyres suggest the date may be the early 1920s. This was the period of the Wembley Exhibition (1924-25) with its British Lion postal cancellation and the postal slogan 'British Goods Are Best'.

In May 1933 Burton staged a Civic Week to 'foster the interests of the inhabitants and attract the outside world'. Events included a procession of decorated trade vehicles, barrel pushing, dances, plays, an elaborate river carnival, Sir Alan Cobham's Air Display, Scout and Guides gala, a military pageant, gramophone recitals in Stapenhill bandstand, visits to local industries and a shop window dressing competition in three categories, things to use, wear and eat. This Co-operative Society branch entered the third section and one trusts that the judges arrived before this finely balanced display took a knock!

Two successive royal occasions in the mid-1930s produced the customary celebrations around the town, with colourful souvenir programmes detailing local events and commemorations. May 1935 was the Silver Jubilee of King George V and Queen Mary; May 1937 saw the Coronation of King George VI and Queen Elizabeth. On one of these occasions this happy group of little girls, each with a flag to wave, was photographed in the playground at St Peter's School, Stapenhill, now the Bridge Surgery.

Burton councillors assembled to inspect the town's first double-decker bus, FA 7948, which was one of two wartime utility Guy Arab models allocated to the town on 3 November 1943. They went on a test drive the next day. Additional buses arrived in 1944, helping to relieve local transport problems and replacing some outdated single-deckers. The importance of public transport at this time is demonstrated by the figure of 11,728,051 passengers carried during 1944. This pioneer vehicle, twice rebuilt, was scrapped in 1961. At one time fears had been expressed that double-deckers could be blown over while crossing Trent Bridge.

The Home Guard, formed as Local Defence Volunteers on 14 May 1940, officially stood down from 1 November 1944 but final parades were on Sunday 3 December. The 8th Staffs (Burton) Battalion was represented in London by Sgt R.H. Watts and Privates A.E. Lester and A.F. Claxton who paraded in Hyde Park where King George VI took the salute. In Burton the battalion assembled at Peel Croft, marched to King Edward Place and onto Horninglow Street where the Commander, Lt-Col S.R. Sharp MM, took the final salute outside the drill hall. The battalion was finally dismissed after a drumhead service in High Street.

As Britain slowly recovered from the dark days of the Second World War, the accession of the young Queen Elizabeth in 1952 heralded a new optimism. The press talked of 'the dawn of a new Elizabethan age' and children were predictably described as 'young Elizabethans'. This class of forty-one at Grange Street Junior School was just such a group. They are costumed for a traditional Christmas pantomime, *Babes in the Wood*. Many things were still in short supply and school equipment was scarce so that programmes were drawn and coloured by the class and collected in again after each performance ready for the next audience. Aided by a surviving copy, Sheila Crisp can be picked out as Robin Hood and there will surely be others who will recognize themselves and friends, perhaps recalling lines and songs and all the fun of this colourful show.

Post-war nationalization of the electricity industry brought plans for a power station at Drakelow. Nearness to fuel supplies and the Trent made it an ideal site. Stage one began in 1950 with a rail link to the Burton to Leicester line, which is splendidly in view here. 'A' station was finished in 1955 followed by 'B' and 'C' to complete Europe's largest coal-fired power station by 1966. From the top of the new construction are Stapenhill (R), Burton (L), Scalpcliffe and Waterloo Clump straight ahead. Thousands watched the demolition of four Drakelow cooling towers on 20 December 1998.

Few changes made greater impact on the town than the end of the brewery railway and other internal rail systems from the 1960s. Tracks were cleared and premises swept away in the following decades, opening out areas which had been warrens of industrial buildings and sidings with obscure branch lines meandering among them. R. Jeffcoat was one photographer who captured the final days of such scenes as this on the Midland Bond End branch. James Street signal box controlled this part of the network.

Steam ended on British Railways in 1968 but in September 1974 the Pacific locomotive *Sir Nigel Gresley* passed through Burton. This was the hundredth LNER Pacific to be built. Named after its distinguished designer, it is preserved in working order. The visit attracted the cameras of local enthusiasts. Sir Nigel, born at Netherseal Rectory, was buried in Netherseal churchyard in 1941. Burton engine sheds closed in 1966 and are now totally demolished but here they partly survive, enclosed by a breeze-block wall built by Lloyds when they were using the building as a pattern store.

This is a picture that will stir many memories. It shows the interior of the old Burton Baths, which closed at 5.00 p.m. on 9 March 1980 for the last time and were subsequently demolished. The baths were presented to the town in 1875 by Richard and Robert Ratcliff. There were later alterations and additions including Turkish baths, from 1903 until 1951, and a sauna suite. There was also an extraordinary steam-filled room that made one think of Heath Robinson, which was the Corporation laundry. In Edwardian days local enthusiasts pioneered the game of water polo here.

The closure of Greensmith's mill in May 1991 ended activity on one of the town's most historic sites. A Burton corn mill probably existed even before the Norman Conquest. It passed into abbey control and then remained continuously in use, although electricity was subsequently employed and low river levels affected its water power. This photograph shows nineteenth-century machinery at the time of closure. Regrettably it was removed and broken up. Buildings on the adjoining island figured in Burton's industrial past as fulling, cotton, forging and flint mills. (Photograph by permission of C. Pipes, PWS Photography, Swadlincote: ref 50/1).

While this book was being compiled familiar landmarks continued to disappear, including the ancient tree giving its name to Beech House, Stapenhill. After removal in November 1998 a ring count dated it back into the eighteenth century, an age of around 206 years. This view from around 1900 shows traces of huge lower branches long since removed. The tree had overlooked the Grand Bazaar and Opening Ceremony of Stapenhill Institute (opposite) in 1888 and looked down Main Street to an even older background – the old Punch Bowl Inn and the roofs and outbuildings of Stapenhill House.

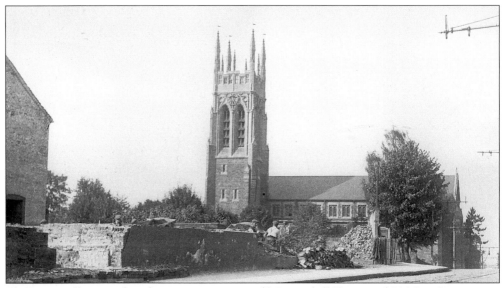

This picture illustrates how history can repeat itself. Stapenhill House and 90 Main Street, once the vicarage, were demolished in 1932 for Stapenhill Gardens to be laid out. Tramlines unused since 1929 still remained in the road, as well as evidence of continuing horse traffic. The tram standards themselves remained as lamps until well after the Second World War. Just over fifty years later one could photograph an almost identical scene as the middle portion of Stapenhill Gardens was bulldozed for access to the new St Peter's Bridge. Work for this project started in February 1984.

The first plan for Burton's second river crossing was prepared in 1865, when Stapenhill Road turnpike was still shown on the map. St Peter's Bridge finally opened to the public on Sunday 30 June 1985. This was a gala occasion, celebrating a wait of 120 years, before it opened for traffic. Thousands paid £1 for charities and walked across to sign a register. This photograph shows Burton's then oldest inhabitant, Mrs Alice Thornley, aged 103, signing her name. She could recall the Stapenhill ferry boat prior to Ferry Bridge opening in 1889.

The 1990s have seen Burton Infirmary swept away with the completion of the new Queen's Hospital. This is the first New Street frontage but by the time it was demolished many of the original buildings of 1899 had been altered, enlarged or rebuilt. The later frontage here absorbed several of the small properties seen on the right, which included Warr's first newsagent's shop and the Fish and Quart. The rebuilt ground floor block opened in 1931. Beyond can be seen the turret of the Baptist church, now the Comet site, which was destroyed by fire in March 1966.

Along with the infirmary, associated properties disappeared with the almost total clearance of Union Street. The demolished nurses' home opened on 6 March 1931 and was named Holford House after one of the infirmary's leading surgeons. On the corner of Duke Street was the former maternity and gynaecological unit, recorded in this busy period photograph. It was previously known as the Nursing Institute, which was founded around 1884 to provide nurses, maternity and medical advice for the needy, as well as some accommodation for nursing staff. Opposite, only the Burton Union inn and the former basket shop survive from old Union Street.

I hope it is not too late to wish you "A happy New Year" P.E.P.

Jan 18. 1901

These two items return us to where the chapter began. The twentieth century heralded the golden age of picture postcards and the great enthusiasm for collecting them, providing us today with invaluable images of past times. Early cards were court size, as in this example which bears a Queen Victoria stamp dated four days before her death. The message had to be written on the picture side. Larger size postcards were permitted from November 1899 but the message was still shared with the picture until 'divided back' cards arrived in 1902, allowing both message and address on the back.

This is an early photographic card of the 'divided back' type, advising that half the back 'may now be used for communication'. This allowed a full size scene on the front to be appreciated, in this case a panorama of the Burton of 100 years ago. Nearly all the prominent buildings in this view have gone, along with the town's innumerable chimneys and the smoke they generated. Had the wind been westerly rather than northerly the photographer, Siddals of Newhall, could hardly have achieved such a fine clear picture, but the great contrast is with the restricted panoramic view of the court card above.

Two
Mid-Victorian Christmas

Discovering aspects of everyday life and happenings in Burton and the social background of earlier times becomes possible after the publication of the first local newspapers. Weekly editions from the mid-1850s allow us to spotlight revealing cameos of the local scene at a particular time, such as Christmas in mid-Victorian Burton and district.

Most noticeable at this time is the absence of anything relating especially to Christmas until around a fortnight before and then, apart from conventional reflections about the New Year, very little is reported afterwards apart from court cases dealing with those who misbehaved.

Christmas benevolence received rightful publicity in announcements such as: 'We, the (13) undersigned grocers have agreed to close our respective establishments on Tuesday 24 December (1861) in order to give our young men and apprentices an opportunity of visiting their friends at Christmas' and 'All the drapers of Burton upon Trent have agreed to close their establishments on 23 and 24 December.' Plainly people were quite prepared to manage without the last minute panic shopping that seems to be the vogue today.

It became customary for newspapers to publish particulars of seasonal gifts provided for employees. In 1864, for example, Bass & Co. distributed over 1,400lbs of beef to their men and large quantities of game to their clerks. Salt & Co. gave each man a joint of beef and likewise Thornewill and Warham, the engineers. It was the equivalent of around 3d per pound to buy in Burton Christmas market. Thompson & Son gave their employees a supper and 5s each. Mr Evershed also invoked the subtle social status symbol of beef for his men and game for his clerks. At the Union Workhouse each inmate was regaled on Christmas Day with roast beef, plum pudding, plum cake, tea, tobacco and ale; the latter also provided by Mr Evershed. The large red brick building in Horninglow Street accommodated 300 paupers and this Christmas meal would contrast greatly with normal workhouse fare. Dinners and 'good ale' were given to 100 Bretby Colliery miners.

Other Burton Christmas Market prices were the approximate equivalent of 6p per lb for butter; 10 eggs for 5p; chickens 12 to 16p per couple; geese expensive at around 25p each; no turkeys offered. Cheese was under 3p per lb; bacon 2 to 3p; ham and lamb 3 to 4p with mutton slightly less; veal and pork around 3p; codfish 2p; herrings 5p for 2 dozen; and flour just under 10p per stone. For those who could afford it I.J. Close, the wine and spirit merchant of Station Street, advertised Best Old Port, 1847 vintage, for 8s per bottle; Best Old Sherry 4s; Moet & Chandon best champagne 7s; Hennessey's Old Pale Cognac Brandy 4s 10d; Old Scotch Whiskey 3s 6d; Fine Old Jamaica Rum 3s 4d; and Best London Gin 2s 6d.

By 1861 an editorial was commenting that 'Christmas trees have become a great attraction. Each branch laden with amusing articles, sweets and twinkling festal lights [naked candles] the Christmas tree in the midst of a group of bright eyed children forms a great source of delight.'

Mrs Lowe's Fancy Depository at 165 Horninglow Street, next to the Bell Hotel, advertised: 'Christmas Trees and Juvenile Parties – articles for trees may now be seen. A Christmas tree will be on view on Monday next.' Her notice appeared, ironically, on 14 December 1861, the day that Prince Albert died. He had introduced the Christmas tree to this country after his marriage to Queen Victoria in 1840.

Mid-Victorian Station Street at its junction with High Street, c. 1860. Until 1868 it remained little more than a cart lane twenty feet wide, including a footway, and still containing properties from its day as Cat Street. Initially, only the name changed with the coming of the railway in 1839. The 1868 development made it thirty-three feet wide and in the early 1900s it assumed its present width, although a few cottages actually survived until Coronation Buildings were erected in 1953.

Mrs Lowe announced that she was receiving novelties from London and Paris suitable for presentation over the Christmas season. Her selection included chess sets, draughts, games for youths, juvenile tool chests, drawing cases, writing desks, work boxes in assorted woods or papier mâché as well as ladies' jewellery, real jet ornaments, flower-scented toilet soaps and other toilet requisites.

Mr Whitehurst in High Street offered playing cards, photographic albums, cartes de visite *and Christmas cards in 1862. Although Christmas cards became available in the 1840s they were not produced in great quantities until Tuck's cards appeared in the 1870s. For personal* carte de visite *or album portraits J. Simnett's Portrait Rooms could be visited where the cost was 8s 6d a dozen.*

A novel alternative Christmas gift could be a visit to Simnett's Temperance Hotel at 190 Station Street to consult Mr J. Pasquoll, the practical phrenologist, with reference to character and choice of trade or profession by examination of the skull. The terms were: verbal, children 6d, adults 1s; analysis of character 2s 6d upwards. Advice was also given on matrimony.

Another Christmas option announced: 'Persons wanting feathers or feather beds, pure and clean, will do well to make an immediate application at Coe's Furniture Warehouse, 52/53 Station Street.' This was no doubt the result of plucking Christmas poultry. A new bed to go with new feathers was on offer from Mr G. Webster, the brass and iron bedstead maker, with prices from 10s 6d upwards. He also advertised gas chandeliers, pendants and brackets. Burton gasworks had opened in 1832 near the corner of Union Street, moving to Wetmore in 1872. For many people though, Christmas would be cosily lamplit. John Lucas of 69 High Street supplied best paraffin at $12\frac{1}{2}$p per gallon and complete paraffin lamps from 4p each. Fine French Colza (rape) oil for moderator lamps was sold in 10 gallon tins at 23p per gallon.

Christmas travel for local visits was available from Charles Beard at the Fox and Goose. Parties to station from all parts of town, 5p; country, 5p per mile. Saddle horses, gigs and phaetons, over six miles, at 4p per mile. For rail travellers the Midland Railway's new St Pancras station, with its cellar storage for Burton beers, did not open until 1868. Before that, Midland trains ran from Bedford to Hitchin and via the Great Northern Railway into King's Cross, usually much delayed. Trains departing Burton at 7.55 a.m. reached Leicester at 9.25. The 9.45 from Leicester was then due in King's Cross at 1.40 p.m.

You could get your teeth into good order for the Christmas festivities by visiting Messrs Crapper and Brierley, Surgeon Dentists, who attended at Lomas' Chemist shop in High Street. They stopped decaying teeth with enamel silica cement, which was the exact colour of tooth, at a cost of 25p. Stopping a tooth with gold also cost 25p while silver cost 8p. A single, warranted, artificial tooth cost 50p but commoner qualities were from 12 ½ p. A new set of mineral teeth cost from £10 and American teeth £4.

Ordish and Hall, then in High Street, were calling the attention of ladies to special lines in counterpanes, ticks, calicos, umbrellas and stays. George Douglas, silk mercer, listed a fascinating selection of fabrics of the day: Black French Merinos, Panamattas, Balmoral Crapes, Poplins, Barathras, Reps, Coburgs and Alpacas. There were bargain lines in straw bonnets as they were out of season.

Tuesday 27 December 1864 was chosen for laying the foundation stone of St John's church, Horninglow. A vellum describing the new church was deposited in a bottle with coins of the realm and a copy of the Burton Times and sealed up in a cavity. There was a large attendance, which was hardly surprising with little happening over the Christmas season and, as yet, few organized sporting events. At Stafford, however, you could have joined a crowd of over 8,000 to watch the public execution of two men outside Stafford Gaol. Burtonians had to wait for the full, detailed press report alongside that of the St John's church ceremony.

That scene aptly leads into demonstrating another side of mid-Victorian Christmases with a brief look at a few more of the unhappy ghosts of Christmas past whose troubles were always enthusiastically elaborated for newspaper readers. There was at least leniency for little Anne Goodhead, aged six, and her sister Rose, five, who were charged with stealing a 16lb cheese. Sgt Kelly proved his case but the Bench discharged them on account of their ages. It is a wonder how two little girls manoeuvred, concealed or conveyed a 16lb cheese.

Looking down Station Street towards High Street shows that it still mainly comprised small terraced houses. Shops and commercial premises were principally concentrated in High Street, Horninglow Street and around the Market Place, extending along into Lichfield Street. New Street, though much wider, also still contained many terraced cottages similar to these. However, recent improvements here have included paving and the occasional gas lamp, although this picture does illustrate the poor condition of roads at this time.

In spite of the emergence of shopping, commercial and brewery premises and some good town houses (examples of which survive), High Street also had cottage properties remaining from earlier days, most with outside shutters to close over the windows at night. The houses here were demolished when Bass' railway crossing was made. Previously floaters had used a narrow gateway just discernible on the left. From 1860 Burton's elaborate network of brewery railways and those of the Midland Railway began to snake across the streets, creating the numerous crossings for which the town became notorious.

Lydia Betteridge, a servant girl aged thirteen, was less fortunate. Charged with theft from her employer, John Dickinson, she was committed to the House of Correction for fourteen days. Sarah Lea, a tramp, was charged with bad language, drunkenness and breaking windows. With no money to pay damages and costs she was dispatched to gaol for fourteen days over Christmas. 'A miserable looking man who either could or would not speak' was charged under the Vagrancy Act with sleeping in Mr Outram's ash pit. He received fourteen days with hard labour. Three men who removed night soil at an improper hour were luckier when they were charged with an offence against the Town Act. They were fined 2½p each and 38p costs.

One has to feel slightly sorry for a gentleman called Thomas from Church Gresley whose little outing to Burton was not an unqualified success. Mary Ann Barnes, 'a nymph of the pave' was charged with stealing 62½p from Thomas' purse. Shortly before Christmas in 1863 he was induced to accompany her to her lodgings and while upstairs his purse was removed from his coat pocket. Mary Ann was committed to the House of Correction for three calendar months.

It is also interesting to note that the watchful eye of the law was already on road users. John Chapman was charged with driving his horse and cart furiously in Moor Street. Witnesses, however, believed that his speed was not above six or seven miles per hour. The Bench agreed that this hardly represented furious driving so they dismissed the charge.

Although not a lot of village news found its way into the early papers, there are a few interesting Christmas items such as the case of Thomas Villiers of the Queen Adelaide inn at Woodville who had the misfortune to drop down dead while feeding his pig on Christmas Day 1862. The inquest verdict was 'That deceased died by the visitation of God'. At Yoxall in 1859 John Snape died peacefully just before Christmas aged ninety-eight, but deprived of his ambition to help ring the bells of Yoxall church for his seventy-ninth successive Christmas Day.

In 1861 the Yoxall mail cart was unable to reach Branstone post office due to severe flooding. The driver left his cart and nobly carried the mailbags along the canal towpath, unfortunately arriving at Burton just too late for the dispatch of letters that morning. Another popular postman was Jack Shepherd of Hartshorne where the inhabitants presented him with a new suit of clothes and a hat for Christmas in appreciation of his services.

Charles Holloway and James Simkins were charged with stealing two ducks from a pool at Rolleston Hall. The evidence had been eaten but they were found guilty. Holloway's Christmas dinner cost him seven days in Stafford Gaol after Sir Oswald Mosley appealed for leniency as Simkins, he considered, was the ringleader. Simkins received twenty-one days of hard labour. In happier vein, the boys of Wakefield's Charity School, Tutbury, went to Rolleston Hall on Christmas Eve 1861 to sing carols before Sir Oswald and Revd P.P. Mosley. All ninety-four were treated to buns and plum cake before returning to Tutbury and marching through the town, singing at the houses of the principal inhabitants.

In conclusion, something rather unexpected. On Christmas Day 1865 'a most interesting tea and public meeting was held in the New Wesleyan Reform Church at Newhall. Upwards of 300 persons partook of excellent cake and tea. In the evening a public meeting was addressed by various ministers and gentlemen, the choir contributing appropriate pieces to make this one of the pleasantest gatherings ever held in Newhall.' Of all days in the year one thinks of Christmas Day as a family affair normally spent at home or with friends, perhaps in modern times eating out, but certainly not a day to attract hundreds of people from their homes for a double-session public event. It is a far cry from the attractions of Christmas television or being prepared to spend Christmas night on a city pavement in order to secure Boxing Day sale bargains.

You can be forgiven for not immediately recognizing this location. It is a section of mid-Victorian Burton but it was not swept away until the mid-1930s. This is the junction of Park Street, Lichfield Street and Fleet Street. Burton's first automatic telephone exchange has just been opened in Fleet Street in 1933, replacing a block of old properties. Those in the photograph are recorded just before their demolition. A memorable 'common lodging house' survived next to the exchange until the 1960s.

The shop to the left of the Bell Hotel in Horninglow Street was where Mrs Lowe's demonstration Christmas tree was displayed in 1861 with her 'suitable Christmas gifts'. In 1912 the Bell became the Territorial Force headquarters, many Burtonians enrolling here in 1914. The Force became the Territorial Army in 1921. Before the recent move to Hawkins Lane, this was the headquarters for 'C' Company, 1st Battalion, Mercia Volunteers and later also housed No. 351 (Burton) Squadron, Air Training Corps. The surviving frontage is a reminder of one of Burton's principal hotels advertising in 1902, 'good stabling (right), electric light and every modern convenience'.

BRETBY COLLIERIES,						
No. *885*				*Feb 10* 1876		
Mr. *Champ*						
~~Billings~~ *Hatton*						
BOUGHT OF						
The Rt. Hon. A. E. Countess of Chesterfield.						
Description.	Tons.	Cwt.	Price per Ton.	£	s.	d.
Coal Gross Weight	*4*	*14*				
Carriage	*1*	*3*				
	3	*11*	*14/-*	*2*	*9*	*9*
Waggoner *Billings*						

On 10 February 1876 Wagoner Billings collected coal from Bretby Colliery and possibly envied colliery employees who enjoyed 'dinner and good ale' at Christmas as he drove his wagon across the new Burton bridge and out to Hatton. There he delivered 3 tons, 11 cwt of coal priced at fourteen shillings per ton. Bretby Colliery, on Stanton Lane and part of the Earl of Caernarvon's estates, was sunk in 1872 but closed in 1962. In 1876 a 'good miner' at this pit was reported as earning six shillings for eight hours work.

Branston has always been at risk from flooding as a Victorian postman found out. This photograph was taken in December 1910 when a bad inundation affected Burton and surrounding districts, in spite of the construction of the Branston flood bank in 1880. Photographed 'near the station', the railway lines can just be discerned approaching the crossing, which still remains for pedestrians. The actual entrance to Branston station, open from 1889 until 1930, was by steps from the main road bridge.

Yoxall church was where John Snape helped to ring in Christmas for seventy-nine successive years. The church of his day was extensively rebuilt in 1868 but retained its seventeenth-century tower and memorials to the Ardens of demolished Longcroft Hall; and of the Welles family who lived in a moated manor house replaced by Hoar Cross Hall. Simnett has given this scene interest by waiting for a local white-coated tradesman to drive past in his trap.

Rolleston Hall's former grounds are a reminder of the poaching activities of Messrs Holloway and Simkin, filching two of Sir Oswald Mosley's ducks for Christmas dinner. Earlier, in his *History of Tutbury* (1832), Sir Oswald recorded the lively adventures of a truly professional poacher named Willard. He lived at Tatenhill Gate and long outwitted local gamekeepers. No ducks for him, though, as his speciality was deer from the Needwood Forest estates. This bridge, now on a public footpath, survives though with railings replacing stonework. There are still ducks in the area.

In his short *History of Tutbury* (1887) H. Whittaker has little to say about the Victorian town itself but his booklet does contain this interesting view of the Castle House as it was until altered early in the Victorian period. It was erected around 1750 from remains of the timber-framed King's Lodging of 1631-35. The present porch replaced the one shown in the engraving; a hexagonal projection with three arched openings, gothic two-light windows on the first floor and crowned by a parapet with battlements.

Three

Theatre Royal
Newton Solney

Until the opening of St George's Hall in December 1867, Burton's old Market Place town hall was the principal venue for concerts and recitals directed towards the district's 'carriage folk'. Light entertainment and plays were usually staged in rooms attached to public houses with entrance through the hostelry. Consequently they were not much frequented by the gentry and certainly not by the ladies of the family. There was thus scope for amateur dramatics, which enjoyed great popularity during the nineteenth century.

Readers of Jane Austen's novels may recall that family theatricals feature in Mansfield Park where Sir Thomas Bertram is amazed at returning home and finding his billiard room transformed into a theatre. Because such occasions were normally for purely private amusement, factual records are scarce but we do have a record of an event at Christmas 1855 which took place at the Theatre Royal, Newton Solney. This was the title given for the evening to one of the large rooms at Newton Park which, at this time, was a residence of the Worthington family, the Burton brewers.

On Twelfth Night family, friends and villagers were invited to attend a grand entertainment, rehearsed over the Christmas period, which we only know about because someone suggested having miniature posters printed by way of invitation. They were designed in the manner of professional theatrical playbills from those days. The copy shown here has had to be transcribed from a fragile original which was retained as a souvenir. The 'company' comprises members of the Worthington family and friends and formed a finale to the celebrations of the Christmas season.

The head of the family at this time was William Worthington (1799-1871) but the best known of the performers is W.H. Worthington (1826-1894). The accompanying photograph shows him later in life but it is not difficult to imagine him as an impressive King Alfred on his appearance at the Theatre Royal.

Newton Park was built in 1798 and subsequently became the home of the Ratcliff family, after which it was converted into a hotel in the 1960s.

Another local occasion recorded from even earlier times is the performance at Bretby House on Twelfth Night 1639 of a masque devised by Sir Aston Cokayne of Ashbourne. The true birth of local amateur dramatics, however, would seem to be Thursday 25 April 1867 when a first entertainment was given by the newly formed Burton-on-Trent Amateur Dramatic Society as a result of 'a few gentlemen of the town assiduously working to found such a group'.

```
         THEATRE ROYAL, NEWTON SOLNEY.
         ──────────────
    IMMENSE ATTRACTION!  UNPARALLELED SUCCESS!
         ──────────────
  Engagement for a Short Time of old Favourites:
            Miss Emily Gillett
    Mr. Albert Worthington     and
         Mr. Frank Worthington,
      Also the Celebrated Pianist
         Mr. Henry Parsons.

  ON  TUESDAY  EVENING  JANUARY  6th.  1856 -
      will be Performed the admired play
            A L F R E D  ! ! !

  Alfred  (King of England) Mr. W.H. Worthington
  Grubbs  (a Farmer)         Mr. A.Worthington
  Gandelin (His wife)       Miss Emily Gillett
  Ella (an Officer)          Mr. J. Worthington
         Mr. Henry Parsons
            after which
  having been engaged at an immense expense to the
  management, will perform several well-known pieces
              on the piano.
         ──────────────
    The whole to conclude with the laughable
    farce of B L I N D   M A N ' S   B U F F!
    in which the whole strength of the Company
              will appear.
         ──────────────
    Stage Manager and Director: Mr. Worthington
    Box Keeper                   Mr. Parsons

  Doors open at half-past Seven and the Performance to
            commence at Eight o'clock.
  The free list is suspended on account of the heavy
  outlay attendant upon the engagement of so many
  stars of the first magnitude.
            GOD SAVE THE QUEEN
  January 3rd., 1856.
```

A transcribed copy of the Newton Park playbill. Without the survival of a fragile and faded original, details of this interesting occasion could well have been lost.

William Henry Worthington was one of the stars of the play. This is a much later portrait taken when he was prominent in local affairs. Chairman of the Town Commissioners, he became Burton's first mayor after the town became a municipal borough in 1878. Following his death in 1894, control of the Worthington brewery passed to the Manners family.

Newton Park was built for Abraham Hoskins in 1798 but the Worthingtons lived there from 1836 until the death of William Worthington (senior) in 1871. Towards the end of the century the house was acquired by Robert Ratcliff and substantially redesigned. This is an Edwardian rear view from the garden. The house was again converted and opened as a hotel in 1966. The long room under the awning, which became a dining room, could well have been used as the Theatre Royal.

Pictures of estate workers are fairly scarce but this is a scene of poultry keeping in Newton Park around 1908. The young man is recorded as being a son of the family and is lending a hand with the birds. 'It is taken early in the morning when they are having the sitting hens off.' There were at least six long sets of nesting boxes so that feeding, watering, egg collecting and rehousing, no doubt after free-ranging all day, would make for busy daily tasks.

In Newton itself, villagers watch a meet of the Meynell Hunt outside the Unicorn Inn. This was a regular Meynell fixture when covering this part of South Derbyshire. The date was Wednesday 5 March 1908 and Pentlow Page, son of landlord Alfred Page, sent the postcard to his auntie telling her all about it and that he had drawn a fox on the paper she sent him. Whether the Meynell drew a fox or not, we can't say! Outwardly, the Unicorn is very recognizable but the building to the right has been replaced by a car park.

Worthington's brewery remained independent until 1 January 1927 when Bass and Worthington merged. This period of many amalgamations saw Ind Coope and Allsopp joining forces in 1934. In the half century to 1950, the town's 1900 total of twenty-one breweries was reduced to four. Subsequent changes in brewing technology and processes, along with metal canisters replacing traditional wooden casks, made a great impact on the local scene. The last apprentice cooper was 'trussed out' in 1965. This picture shows Worthington's cooperage around 1930, with foreman cooper H. McCrea seated third from right. Note the comic and other 'pin-up' postcards on the extreme right.

Four
Burton's Mrs Beetons

Few Victorian and Edwardian kitchens would be without a copy of Mrs Beeton's Everyday Cookery Book, that essential guide to the substantial meals of the period. A popular way of raising funds for churches and chapels at a bazaar or sale of work was to offer a book of recipes selling at around sixpence but produced at minimum cost with local parishioners subsidising advertising and the ladies and their friends contributing favourite or unusual recipes. One such example was a 1910 compilation in aid of St. Peter's Church, Stapenhill.

To set the tone the dowager Lady Burton had provided four of her favourite recipes for page one. Maybe we should reserve judgement on whether her cook was involved here or whether her ladyship really did make her own lemonade to serve as an alternative drink to members of the Bass family:

'LEMONADE. Six lemons, 6 oz sugar (lump), 3 qts boiling water; peel rinds into a jug very finely. Squeeze the juice through a strainer, then add sugar and pour the boiling water on top. Let it get quite cold and decant into a glass jug.'

Rolled beef for breakfast was contributed by Miss S. Cubley of 87 Horninglow Street. It may not appeal to every reader as an ideal breakfast dish:

'ROLLED BEEF FOR BREAKFAST. ½ lb beef, ¼ lb ham or bacon, ¼ lb bread crumbs, salt and pepper to taste, a little nutmeg, chopped parsley and thyme. Put meat through mincer and mix altogether with one egg. Tie in a cloth, like roll pudding, and boil for 3 hours. When cold roll in bread crumbs.'

This breakfast delicacy was obviously embarked on the previous evening. Next, Mrs G. Morland Day's recipe firstly required a pair of ptarmigan, 'a species of grouse with feathered toes inhabiting the tops of mountains'. The meal could then be prepared, again starting well in advance:

'STEWED PTARMIGAN. Cut up a brace of ptarmigan into joints, put them into a pie dish, flavour with salt and black pepper, cover with a good gravy and bake for 4 hours. Serve cold in the dish in which it has been baked. The gravy must be rich enough to set in a jelly. The oven should be hot to start the stew (which must be covered with a plate) but let it cool down as soon as the gravy boils, refill the dish occasionally as the gravy wastes in the cooking.'

With an even longer preparation time, Miss S. Thompson of Ivy Lodge, Stapenhill, suggested this variation on traditional Christmas pudding:

'CARROT PLUM PUDDING. Take 8 oz of carrots (grated), 1 lb Boiled potatoes (mashed), 1 lb of flour, same suet, ditto sugar, also raisins and currants, and 4 oz citron, the rind and juice of 1 lemon, nutmeg, and, if liked, 1 tablespoonful of rum. Mix flour, suet, sugar and fruit, etc., well together, then add the grated carrot, and lastly the potatoes (hot); thoroughly mix all the ingredients and boil for 6 or 8 hours. Serve with hot sauce - wine or lemon. Neither milk or eggs are required.'

Next, and provided that you could commence preparation not hours but days in advance, Mrs Bird of 10 Main Street, recommended as her speciality:

'APPLE GINGER. Take apples, after being peeled, cored and quartered, to weigh 4 lbs Make a syrup of 2 lbs of sugar and 1 pint of water. Pour over apples and leave for 2 days. Then boil up with 2 lbs moist sugar, 2 oz bruised ginger tied in a bag, a quarter teaspoonful cayenne, add wineglass of gin, cut up 4 lemons in small pieces and simmer all for 1 hour.'

After waiting all that time for a drink the gin bottle might have been a temptation. This brings us to Miss Brown whose address was Bank House. This was the living accommodation over Lloyds Bank (formerly Burton Old Bank) in High Street where her father had recently retired as manager:

'CHESTNUT BISCUITS FOR TEA. Take 6oz chestnuts weighed after they have been boiled, peeled and pounded, then add a short teaspoonful grated lemon rind, 18 oz castor sugar and stiffly beaten whites of 10 eggs. Mix all well together in a basin, then put the paste on a board and mould it into the required shapes. Bake on paper in a moderate oven. Do not remove the paper until they are cold.'

This is of course the period when many people regarded supper as a fourth meal and Miss E. Thornley of 2 St Peter's Street came up with this suggestion:

'A NICE SUPPER DISH. Take 6 hard-boiled eggs and remove shells, thickly coat them with sausage meat, roll in egg and bread crumbs, and fry in plenty of fat. When cold cut in half.'

And a good night's rest to you after trying that! Finally, among various hints and miscellaneous items was an amusing contribution on how to organize party guests:

'RECIPE FOR AN EVENING PARTY. Take all the ladies and gentlemen you can get, put them into a room with a small fire and stew them well; have ready twelve packs of cards, a piano, a handful of prints and drawings and throw them in from time to time. As the mixture thickens, sweeten with politeness, and season with wit (if you have any), if not, flattery will do as well and is very cheap. When all have stewed for an hour, add ices, jellies, cakes, lemonade, wines.'

This last item came from Mrs Perfect of St Peter's Street whose husband was a printer and bookseller at 204/205 Station Street. He had produced this Stapenhill booklet with all its bright suggestions. For a full scale, costed, Christmas dinner it is interesting to go back to Victorian times and contemplate this menu from a family magazine of the 1880s:

Celery Soup
Cod à la Breme
Boned Quails
Boiled Turkey, Mushroom Sauce
Brussels Sprouts au Jus
Roast Round of Beef
Ox Tongue à la Belgravia
Christmas Pudding, Wine Sauce
Mince Pies, Orange Sponge Jelly

Cost: Soup, fish and game 8 shillings. Turkey, beef and tongue 17s 6d. Vegetables and sauces 2s 7d. Sweets 5s. Total £1 13s 1d.

Perhaps it is not too surprising that advertisements like the following typical example regularly appeared in Victorian and Edwardian newspapers:

'Barrow Evans Cordial Peppermint is particularly recommended for all suffering from Wind, Cholic, Spasms, Lowness of Spirits, Indigestion, Nervousness, Bowel Complaints, Loss of Appetite, Palpitation of the Heart, Weakness and Disturbed Sleep. Agent for Burton-on-Trent, Mr Whitehurst, Stationer, The Post Office, High Street.'

This is the formal notice to shareholders of the Burton Union Bank Limited of the meeting which confirmed disposal of the company to Lloyds Bank as from 1 January 1899. The bank was established on 11 October 1839 with around 200, mostly local, shareholders. Branches had been opened at Uttoxeter and Ashbourne and it became the Burton, Uttoxeter and Ashbourne Union Bank with premises in the Market Place before removing to High Street, where the Old Bank building is still Lloyds Bank. Mr Brown continued as manager, perhaps enjoying his daughter's chestnut biscuits with his cup of tea.

THE BURTON UNION BANK, LIMITED.

NOTICE IS HEREBY GIVEN, that an Extraordinary General Meeting of this Company will be held at the Old Bank, Burton-on-Trent, on Monday, the Twentieth day of February, 1899, at 1-15 o'clock in the Afternoon, when the following Resolutions, which were passed by the requisite majority at the Extraordinary General Meeting of the Company, held on the Second instant, will be submitted for confirmation as Special Resolutions :—

RESOLUTIONS.

That the Agreement by this Company, for the sale of the business and assets of the Company to Lloyds Bank, Limited, as from the 1st January, 1899, (a copy whereof has been read to the Meeting, and is identified by the signature of the Chairman thereto,) be approved and adopted

That for the purpose of giving effect to the said Agreement for sale, this Company be voluntarily wound up, and that Messrs. Howard Lloyd and Edwin Atkin Brown be and they are hereby appointed Liquidators thereof without remuneration, and that the same Liquidators be and they are hereby directed to adopt the said Agreement, and do all things necessary for carrying the same into effect.

By Order of the Board,

E. A. BROWN,

General Manager.

Burton-on-Trent,

2nd February, 1899.

James Campbell was a leading local fish, game and poultry dealer at 91/92 High Street, with a branch at Station Street until the total rebuilding there early in the century. He was also an ice merchant with cold storage, although his extensive stock is displayed open to the street. He offered a weekly price list with free deliveries by 'bicycle, errand carts and motor' with special terms for hotels and functions. Specialities included best native oysters, cream and cream cheese and the famous Cambridge sausages. This shop became Mac Fisheries in the early 1930s.

The shop of J.C. Perfect who printed the St Peter's church recipe book. This attractive engraving was included in the *Burton Red Book* (1912), an informative combination of almanac and local gazetteer with splendid illustrations and examples of Perfect's printing services and of various items sold in the shop including local Goss heraldic porcelain. In 1897 he produced a Burton album, priced one shilling, of sixteen large photographs of the town especially commissioned for the book. He was also publisher of the monthly 'ABC' timetable showing all local train services and fares.

Stapenhill church choirboys photographed at the time the recipe book was on sale. Living at 94 Clay Street during the same period was Walter Bullock, a self-taught musician and composer. Born near Fauld, he was a miller at Tutbury before farming at Hanbury. He wrote many hymn tunes, each one named after villages such as Stapenhill where he had played the church organ. They were published in 1913. His music room in Clay Street was a rendezvous for many local musicians.

Five
Night Soil Carts and Roundabouts

A name associated throughout the country with fairgrounds and funfairs was that of Orton and Spooner of Burton upon Trent who manufactured and decorated a wide range of equipment and amusements. Examples of their work could be found wherever fairs were set up and often the showmen's caravans were also the firm's products. They were pioneers of prefabrication because of the need for easy erection, dismantling and conveyance of travelling entertainment.

George Orton was a wheelwright, coach and carriage builder in Princess Street from around 1875. He was associated with C.J. Spooner from around 1894 although the two firms only completely amalgamated in 1925. Their joint works was established in Victoria Crescent where they specialized in building fairground equipment, with its associated carving and gilding, until the 1950s. They diverted into other work during the two world wars. Later they diversified into engineering and industrial products before closure in 1981.

Charles John Spooner's story had its beginnings with the Swan Inn, owned by the Spooner family and originally housed in what became the sub-post office at the foot of Bearwood Hill. In the Swan yard was a tobacco pipe manufactory which C.J. Spooner took over in 1892, starting work as a wood carver and employing two men in his Swan Works. The present Swan Hotel came into being after tenders were invited 'for the erection of a Public House and Premises at Bridge End' in 1867.

In 1898 Spooner moved to Meadow Road, off Trent Bridge. Here, the former storeroom built in 1784 by the Burton Boat Company for the river navigation had become a brewery in 1868, used first by Boddingtons and then by Everards. When Everards moved, Spooner relocated his Swan Works taking with him the name he had used from his beginnings in the Swan Hotel yard. Some of his carvers used Meadow Road until the 1930s.

In addition to their association with fairground products, Orton and Spooner shared joint ownership of the skating rink in Curzon Street which they subsequently converted into the Picturedrome. They were also partners in the Regent Cinema at Derby Turn.

The pictures that follow illustrate some aspects of the story of this notable partnership.

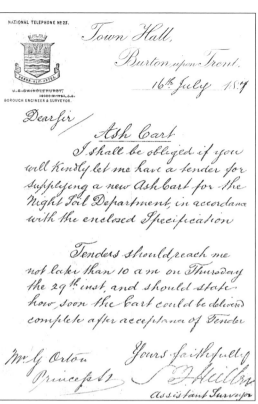

Town Hall,
Burton upon Trent.
16th July 189

Dear Sir/

Ash Cart
 I shall be obliged if you will kindly let me have a tender for supplying a new Ash Cart for the Night Soil Department, in accordance with the enclosed Specification

 Tenders should reach me not later than 10 a m on Thursday the 29th inst, and should state how soon the Cart could be delivered complete after acceptance of Tender

Mr G Orton
Princes St

Yours faithfully
J. F. Miller
Assistant Surveyor

George Orton's premises for carriage and van building were at 95 Princess Street but some of his earlier work was far less exotic than items with which he was subsequently associated. This letter from the Borough Engineer's Department, dated 1897, concerns an ash cart for night soil removal. Even with the approach of the twentieth century there were many local properties not on mains sewerage and the borough's night soil men needed new carts for their rounds of the town's Victorian privies, some of which still stood after the Second World War.

A view illustrating the beginnings of C.J. Spooner's career. The later post office clock can be seen on the building which was the tavern run by the Spooner family before the Swan Hotel was built. C.J. Spooner's original Swan Works was in the rear yard. The Spooners also ran the post office and hired out pleasure craft from these boathouses immediately below Trent Bridge and a gate gave handy access from across the road. These were water sheds where heavier clinker-built boats were backed in and kept immersed to prevent drying out.

An early example of a fairground 'galloper' with Spooner's publicity board. Of interest here are the additions inked in on the original photograph as modifications or suggestions for a new design. These early types with down-pointing legs were called 'Dobbies' but Spooner's carvers soon produced more flowing and realistic animals. A pole position is marked and these were the popular two-seater 'gallopers' which featured on many roundabouts, later often replaced by scenic rides featuring motor cars, dragons and peacocks (in 1922/23), dolphins, geese or speedway motorcycles, offering wide scope for the firm's carvers and painters.

Responsible firms test their equipment and here employees thoroughly enjoy a new helter-skelter. C.J. Spooner has now moved his Swan Works to Meadow Road and this scene is in his yard opposite the works, alongside the river. It is suggested that the figure with the straw hat could be Mr Spooner himself. One of these helter-skelters went to the Britannia Pier, Great Yarmouth, in time for the 1909 Bass trip. Stored in this yard for many years was Spooner's mock up of the Lord Burton statue, tried out on various sites around town before the final choice of the town hall square.

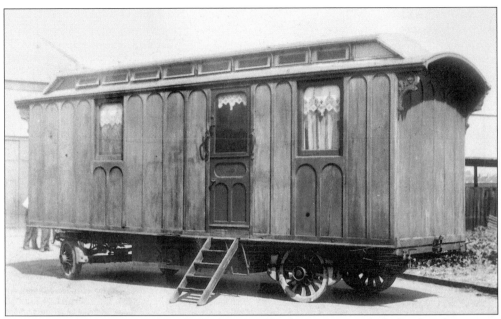

Two contrasting examples of Orton-built vans. The first is a typical, fairly plain but roomy travelling showman's caravan with a long clerestory roof for additional light and air. It has minimal outside carving or decoration but is elaborately finished inside. The second vehicle, however, is a fine demonstration of the wood carver's skills applied to a caravan of traditional design. The location is not known but the smart owner is presumably a travelling wicker chair maker and mender, with his wares in a rack on the roof. He is equally a craftsman in his own right as illustrated by the elaborate specimen from his stock. An Orton and Spooner caravan has been fully restored for the Avoncroft Museum, near Bromsgrove.

Relph and Pedley's electrically driven and lighted motor scenic ride was constructed by Savages of King's Lynn. It was built up in Orton and Spooner's works in Burton for the motor cars, carving and decorating to be added. There is a good view of the mechanical organ. One organ supplier was Gavioli and Company of Paris who had a factory at Manchester to supply British firms. In 1908 Orton and Spooner produced their 'Great Show' with a 120-key Marenghi organ and extensive and revolutionary coloured lighting effects.

Charles Spooner was much in demand for the elaborate carving and gilding which decorated the fronts of bioscope shows and the organs which accompanied these popular attractions early in the century. There is a wealth of decorative work and other features in this photograph of Anderton and Rowland's Grand Empire Palace Bioscope. Power was generated by a built-in steam engine on the right and the organ is positioned on the left. A top-hatted MC, clowns and showgirls are ready to welcome patrons.

Highly specialized and meticulous construction work is in progress here on a wall of death sideshow. The circular wooden structure had narrow slats for spectators to view motorcyclists who took off from a base curved like a basin and, as speed increased, ascended the wall. Riders were sometimes blindfolded or carried a lady passenger – and in one instance, a lion! Orton and Spooner also manufactured dodgem tracks, scenic railways and big dippers which all displayed elaborate carving, gilding and highly coloured painted scenes.

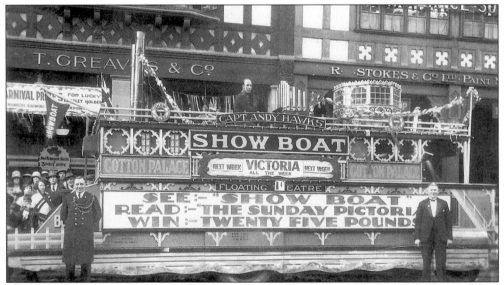

This picture reveals yet another aspect of the firm's work: sets and advertising floats for the film industry. The musical *Show Boat* was staged at Drury Lane in 1928, making a star of Paul Robeson with his song *Old Man River*. After this popular show was made into a film an advertising model was sent on tour. It included an authentic calliope or steam organ, visible on top. The photograph was taken in Chesterfield but clearly readable on the side appears 'G. Orton, Sons and Spooner, Makers, Burton on Trent', an inscription Burtonians were always proud to point out.

Six

The Servants' Christmas Ball

This occasion was recorded by Charles King, a Burtonian who had emigrated to Australia. Recalling events before the First World War, he has left us a little cameo of a way of life that no longer exists: the servants' Christmas ball at Byrkley Lodge. The large house is now a garden and shopping centre visited by many people, not only in the gardening season but in great numbers around Christmas time. Before the First World War it was the private, secluded residence of Mr W.A.H. and Lady Noreen Bass.

Charles King numbered some local musicians among his friends, several of whom played in the Opera House orchestra. One Christmas Eve, when there had been snow for the festive season, Mr King was called upon to take some musicians out to Byrkley Park for the annual 'below stairs' party. Billy Clarke with his violin and Sam Newbold, lumbered with a harp, were among those who set off that winter night, probably after second house finished at the theatre.

They duly arrived in the stable yard, unharnessed the horse and enjoyed a splendid repast before the ball commenced. The house party, led by Lady Noreen Bass, along with the many guests who were spending Christmas at Byrkley, then came to join in the grand march which traditionally opened a ball in those days; 'downstairs' following all the correct 'upstairs' procedure. The house party remained for the first dance, the Circassian Circle, for which the opening figure of The Lancers was played; this alternated with a waltz and a change of partners with each change of music. The staff danced with elegant members of society on whom they would be attending during the following days of Christmas celebrations.

Charles King himself 'had the honour and pleasure of dancing with many society beauties not least of whom was the lovely Lady Noreen Bass'. These ladies and their gentlemen then withdrew and the servants' ball continued until around 5.00 a.m. when Mr King and his musicians set off to drive wearily back to Burton.

At the top of Henhurst Hill Mr King realized that they were not moving smoothly as they approached the descent. 'We're heavy on,' he announced, meaning that there was too much weight on the horse's back; no good when about to go down a steep hill. It was then that they realized both Sam Newbold and his harp were missing from the back seat. Returning as far as the Acorn Inn, they found Sam and his harp straddled across the middle of the road in the snow. He was unhurt but his language, it is gathered, was not in keeping with his recent encounter with high society!

Byrkley Lodge was built between 1887 and 1891 on an earlier site for Hamar Bass, Lord Burton's brother, by R.W. Edis and was described as one of the finest modern country houses in England. It contained a magnificent Reception Hall, five spacious reception rooms and, in a new wing recently added, a billiard room and ballroom. There were forty-one bed and dressing rooms (including a nursery wing and a bachelors' wing), eleven bathrooms and extensive domestic offices along with cellars, laundry, electric power station, gasworks, ice house, stables, motor garage and, of course, extensive grounds and park with lakes. Sadly, this fine country house only survived until 1953 when it was demolished less than seventy years from the time it was built.

The power station comprised an engine room with two 70hp steam engines by Siemens, two boilers by Davy Paxman, a cell room containing sixty cells, a coal store, a smith's shop and an office. The gasworks occupied a secluded position and contained a coke house, a gas generating plant fitted with three pairs of retorts, pumping plant, coal store and a gasometer with a capacity of 30,000 cubic feet.

Drinking water from a well was pumped by a 1.5hp Siemens motor to a tank holding 1,500 gallons in the mansion. Water for household purposes came through a filter bed from the lower lake and was pumped by a Buxton and Thornley (of Burton) 4hp steam engine to additional filter beds from where more pumps lifted it to a 16,000 gallon tank in the tower above the house. There was an extra water supply for the gardens and stables. A full drainage system was connected to the estate's own sewage farm.

What about the musicians who provided the accompaniment for this event? We know quite a lot about shows at the Burton Opera House but members of the orchestra or the backstage team often received little publicity. Some of the backstage brigade are mentioned in Denis Stuart's County Borough History (part 2, chapter 8). Thanks to Charles King and another great local trouper, Dick Kelly, the musicians and some of their antics can still be recalled.

At different times the theatre orchestra included Alf Beare, Charlie Elkington (a music teacher), Fred Fitchett, Jim Casey, Harry Scrimshaw (cornet), Percy Dicken, Percy Reddyhoff and Ralph Boydell. There was also Les Inwood, a fine cornet player who declined offers from London bands, W. Stroud who played the trumpet, and Jack Fletcher on double bass of whom it was said, 'He could play and sleep at the same time'.

Perhaps this claim was not so surprising when you consider the daily routine of Billy Clarke. On piece work at Bass' from 6.00 a.m. to 5.00 p.m. he also played the violin six nights a week at the theatre – often for two houses – finishing around 11.00 p.m., before returning to his home in George Street with two or three colleagues 'for a little music'. On Mondays there was often no time for lunch break because this was when incoming artistes rehearsed and the musicians were given their music for the week, marked their cues and tried out new numbers. The pay was around £1 a week for this part-time job: in nearly every instance on top of a full day's work. Billy Clarke later became the conductor.

Dick Kelly personally recalled many of the Opera House musicians of the 1920s when he too worked backstage assisting with lighting. Many Burtonians will mainly remember him, however, as an entertainer in his own right. He recorded how, over 60 years, he performed in 140 local pubs, halls, clubs, chapels and canteens. Many will still recall 'Uncle Dick', that great favourite at children's entertainments and Christmas parties. His son, John Kelly, sometimes assisted prior to moving to a professional stage career in Australia and they skilfully worked all the old gags. Dick, about to do a mind-reading act, entices a 'complete stranger' up on stage – this being John already planted in the audience:

Dick: 'Now you've never seen me before, have you?'
John: 'No, dad.'

One of my own last recollections of Dick Kelly is of him standing in a shop doorway recalling old times for myself and the shop owner while producing a ping-pong ball out of thin air to the amusement of passers-by. At the end of the tale, as we laughed, he departed with a flamboyant wave declaiming, 'Thank you for the use of the hall.'

What wonderful words by which to recall this splendid performer who appears among the accompanying photographs. We are certainly indebted to Dick and to Charles King for leaving us their record of ways of life which have gone forever.

Keene's 1905 photograph of the new Byrkley Lodge, seen with the sun shining through winter trees. Originally Byrkley was one of the four ancient lodges of Needwood Forest: one in each of the four wards into which the forest was divided, Byrkley was the lodge for Tutbury ward and in the past forest courts were held here and forestry officers appointed. It became a country residence and in the 1850s was the home of M.T. Bass MP. The name derives from Thomas de Berkeley who married a daughter of William de Ferrers, Earl of Derby, and served as keeper of Tutbury ward.

The entrance to the stables at Byrkley. The musicians would have driven through the arch on their arrival. There was stabling here for forty-three horses and, subsequently, a garage for three cars with inspection pit. Today's garden centre visitors will recognize parts of this façade still surviving. Among items sold from the stables at the contents sale in July 1952 was a Merryweather forty-eight rung, telescopic, portable fire escape with hoses, standpipes and nozzles for £27; a child's pony-drawn governess cart for £20; a two-wheeled farm cart for £20; and a four-wheeled dray for £10.

Visitors to the house arrived under a stone arched portico, passed through an outer hall and then entered the lofty main hall or saloon with its oak staircase leading up to a first floor gallery via a half landing. In winter a welcoming log fire would burn in the carved marble and oak-panelled chimney piece. R.W. Edis, the architect, had also worked on the royal residence at Sandringham and obviously set out to ensure that one was suitably impressed on entering the mansion.

Soon after the house was built an additional wing was added, its principal feature being this large, ornate ballroom. The servants' ball, however, would no doubt have taken place in their own ground floor accommodation, which was 'quite shut off from the remainder of the house', but was very extensive. It included a 'spacious' servants' hall and a sitting room, in addition to two kitchens and a host of domestic offices and work rooms, among them a brushing room, boot room, ironing room and flower room.

A Simnett photograph of Lady Noreen Bass taken in 1905. She was the fifth daughter of the Earl of Huntingdon and married Mr William A.H. Bass, the only son of Hamar Bass, in 1903 on his return from service in the South African war. Mr Bass succeeded to the baronetcy held by his uncle, Lord Burton, in 1909.

LADY NOREEN BASS.

931

THE "BURTON" STEAM PUMP.

(THORNLEY'S PATENT)

Is now in use for Feeding Boilers, Pumping Hot and Cold Water, Wort, and Beer, Yea
Pressing, Hydraulic Lifts, Fire Engines, Sewage, and various other purposes.

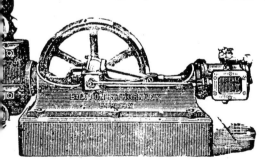

Will pump Hot or Cold Liquor equally we
The simplest and best Pump made. Can
made single-acting if required. These Pate
Steam Pumps are of an entirely new design, a
are offered to the public as the simplest, cheape
and most accessible Steam Pump in the Mark
The Pumps are easily fixed, and can be attend
to by an ordinary workman. All Pumps a
tested with steam and water before being se
out. *⁎* They can be fitted with Air Cylinde
or arranged as Vertical Feed Pumps.

PRICES ON APPLICATION.

The 'Burton' steam pump was used in connection with the Byrkley Lodge water supply. Made by the Burton firm of Buxton and Thornley (whose workforce is shown on p. 94), this example has been preserved and is retained for display at Byrkley Park Garden Centre, where photographs and a model of the house may also be seen.

These final images from Byrkley symbolize both the end of a way of life and the end for many country houses themselves. This is the drawing room at Byrkley Lodge in March 1953 before the auction of fittings and fixtures. The lots indicated are 214, 215 and 217 and include the oak polished parquet floor together with pine floor underneath; ornamental pine panelling; four pairs of carved panelled doors and two plate glass mirrors; and two carved marble chimney pieces with antique cast iron firebacks from around 1690.

The sun shines into the library for nearly the last time. The auction lots here (nos 220, 222 and 223) accounted for the oak polished spring floor, again with pine floor underneath, and a 90ft run of inlaid bookshelves with writing flaps and cupboards in sections, fitted with concealed lighting. Great quantities of books, usually in lots of 20 to 40, had gone previously, generally for less than the equivalent of 5p each: the only lot making big money was James Weatherby's Racing Calendar (1775-1951) at £100.

Some of the Burton Opera House musicians appear here in the theatre, appropriately in a country house setting. Another of the characters from the theatre orchestra recalled by Dick Kelly was Ted Prince who was the percussionist, both there and, later, at the Derby Turn Picture House. As films began to oust stage shows he took on various other jobs, including cycling all round Burton and South Derbyshire when business was bad early in the week to stick 'Enormous Success' slips over the week's theatre posters to drum up business.

We always like to include a typical comic card of the period in our books. It would be wonderful if we could claim that this quite daring Edwardian example was a souvenir of one of the jolly musicians who attended the Byrkley ball. It turned up locally and it was never used, so who knows? Perhaps whoever bought it did have a reason for keeping it!

Dick Kelly, as many older Burtonians will remember him, performing for youngsters at Christmas parties or holiday entertainments. Here he is coaxing a young performer on at the Jubilee Hall in 1963. Musical accompaniment with his piano accordion is by Stan Schofield who is still playing and teaching this versatile instrument. Below, the lightning artist 'Sparti' sketches Dick as he performs at Stapenhill in 1968. On the sheet is Dick's own little nonsense song which youthful audiences would belt out with him, adding the actions:

'Here we are again, happy, bright and gay,
Burton children on a holiday
We don't care if its rains, we don't care if it snows;
And if we catch a cold, all we do is blow our nose!
We don't want any homework, we don't want any sums,
All we want is ice cream, lollipops and gums.
And when I finish my lollipop, you can have the stick,
And then we'll have a sing-song with jolly Uncle Dick.'

Seven
Triumph and Tragedy

This account concerns a young man from Burton, unknown and unremembered today, yet perhaps deserving to be recalled, albeit briefly. This is all that can be done as facts about him are few and far between. Once he was highly proclaimed locally and then, soon after, the curtain came down on a tableau of tragedy.

His name first came to my notice when, in a local shop, I picked up a small gilt-edged volume of poetry with the strange title Miching Mallecho. The author was Paul Richardson and the book was printed and published by John Whitehurst of High Street, Burton upon Trent, in 1857. As regards the title, Paul Richardson knew his Shakespeare and in Act III, Scene ii of Hamlet, the Player King and Queen perform their dumb-show in front of the court. As they exit Ophelia asks Hamlet, 'What means this, my Lord?' His reply is, 'Marry, this is miching mallecho, it means mischief.' According to Brewer's Dictionary of Phrase and Fable the words are from the Spanish and exactly fit Hamlet's setting-up of the mime: 'a bad deed probed by disguised means.'

Paul Richardson's poem fills ninety-four pages of his book. It is a rambling piece mixing political satire, romantic passages, obscure philosophies and the bitter, and occasionally irreligious outpourings of an ardent young rebel against the injustices of society and the establishment. Short poems, often in the same vein, with mankind seeking fraternity, freedom, equality and liberty fill another ninety pages. He was twenty-five when his book appeared, so it is perhaps not unfair to suggest that in his immaturity there is quantity here rather than quality. Few lines stand out as memorable or as quotations of significance although the opening of his poem 'Our Braves' does anticipate the theme of many verses from the period of the First World War:

> 'A tear for the brave who are low in the grave,
> Let them rest for their labor is done!
> A cheer for those who are left with their foes;
> Let them fight till the battle is won.'

The book cost five shillings, which was not cheap in those days. It was a work of limited appeal so that it was almost certainly financed and published privately. We shall see, however, that Mr Whitehurst figures in the Paul Richardson story. He was prominent both as local postmaster and 'copper plate printer' producing one of Burton's first newspapers. Paul's uncle was John Richardson, solicitor, coroner and high bailiff of Burton, also with offices in High Street.

In April 1862 Burton Town Hall, then in the Market Place, was booked for Paul Richardson to read his new works: 'Matty Moor', the 'Miser and Misanthrope'; and 'John Snivelpipe, the Member for Loutsborough'. The Burton-on-Trent Times referred to 'our really clever and talented young townsman'. Regretting a small attendance (prices were three shillings, two shillings and one shilling, again not cheap for those times), it considered that 'the poems possess much merit, abounding with fine passages and exhibiting an amount of poetical ability far above the ordinary twaddle we read nowadays'. The first piece was largely a castigation of religious hypocrisy, 'perhaps a little severe on the religious portion of the community', and the second was a topical and political satire. 'Of his poems he may be justly proud' was the considered summing-up.

Paul Richardson's next public appearance took place just before Christmas 1862 when he delivered a lecture entitled 'Italy, Garibaldi and America'. The Italian patriot Garibaldi was very much in the news at the time and plainly a hero for our republican author with his fervent feelings on freedom and liberty. The Burton Times accorded him a long near-verbatim report running to four full-length columns. The lecture, it said, was 'full of high and generous sentiments ... and an elegant and masterly composition. That our talented townsman is destined to establish a name honourable to himself and to the place of his birth we have little doubt.'

It must have been a happy Christmas then for Paul Richardson, finding himself recognized and acclaimed as something of a big fish in a little local pond. During 1863 and 1864 this newspaper frequently published poems which, although anonymous, are so unmistakably in his style and pattern that they are almost certainly his work. In June 1863 there was a piece in French 'from the English of Paul Richardson'. During 1864 there is a lull with no mention of his name and no more of those distinctive contributions. Then a stark announcement appeared in the 'Deaths' column: '28th November. Mr Paul Richardson, age 32 years.' It was almost two years to the day of his lecture triumph that an obituary notice appeared in The Burton-on-Trent Times:

'It is with feelings of the deepest regret that we have to chronicle the death of our late townsman, Mr Paul Richardson, long known to the public as a contributor to these columns ... The whole neighbourhood seemed enveloped in a dense gloom ... His friends could not at first believe that it was possible he should thus make his exit from the world when he had only just started in the profession of which he was so ardent a lover and to which we have no doubt he would have been an honour had his life been prolonged ... everyone was ready to acknowledge his promptitude and ability as a champion of freedom and liberty. In one of his last contributions to these columns he says, "In one man's life is every man's lesson." How fearfully true he spoke when he implied the world should have a lesson from him. Let us take care the lesson be not lost upon us.'

It was a careful and tactful tribute to follow a tragic suicide. There are many gaps in this story now with only an inquest report to add intrigue to it. Paul Richardson was found dead in bed from a shot wound at a coffee house at 102 High Holborn. Police Sergeant Bailey reported finding in the deceased's pockets about eleven shillings in money, two photographs of women and a pocket book containing a letter written in pencil which said: 'Mother, forgive me; I am only saving you more sorrow. Minnie, forget me; I am not worthy of you! My friends, I have tried you. God! I have wearied you. Finis. Sunday night.'

His patron, Mr Whitehurst, said that he had known Paul for ten years, last seeing him some six weeks ago. He was a solicitor's clerk out of employment and had come up to London with a view to obtaining a situation. He was well connected, his uncle being High Bailiff and coroner for Burton upon Trent. Paul had received £200 from his uncle a fortnight since and £100 previously. He had written to witness from Northampton, stating that he had been fleeced of all his money and requesting the loan of £3 which witnesses granted. The jury returned a verdict of 'Suicide by pistol shot while in an unsound state of mind.'

It will probably never be known why Paul Richardson was out of employment, whether his decision to leave the town was ambition, necessity or retreat. Sadly, it was to be an unhappy Christmas for many people, especially a grieving mother and the shadowy figure of Minnie. Nor can it be said if this artistic young man might have gained distinction for himself and the town.

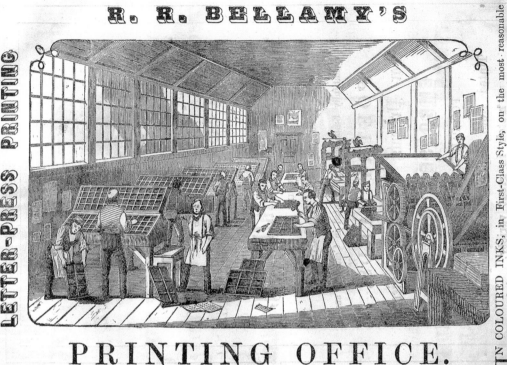

This is a typical printing shop of the period, that of R.R. Bellamy in Bridge Street, Burton, in 1860. From the fifteenth through into the twentieth century, movable metal type was stored in type cases such as those on the left. Letters were then formed into words on a 'composing stick' which could be adjusted to the column width required. Blocks of type were transferred to a tray called the 'galley', which is seen in the centre. Inking and final printing is taking place on the right. After the start of the twentieth century partial automation began with keyboard-controlled machines, both Linotype and Monotype, along with advances in photogravure and offset printing to improve the quality of pictures in newspapers and books. Nowadays press photographs are frequently used for more recent scenes, whereas the pictures of earlier days were recorded by local photographers who then produced souvenirs, often as postcards. R.R. Bellamy was the proprietor and printer of the *Burton Weekly News and General Advertiser* (1856), a newspaper contemporary of the *Burton upon Trent Times and General Advertiser* (1855) produced by Whitehursts who printed and published Paul Richardson's book. From 1852 Bellamy also printed a series of local household almanacs priced at one penny. Almanacs became popular from around 1828, Old Moore's becoming perhaps the best known. Mr Bellamy sang the praises of this local publication in confident verse:

> A Household Calendar complete
> With useful Miscellany;
> Surely no other can compete
> With this by R.R. BELLAMY.

Burton's other newspaper of this period was J. Tresise's *Burton Chronicle* (1860).

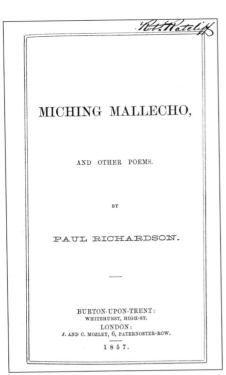

MICHING MALLECHO,

AND OTHER POEMS.

BY

PAUL RICHARDSON.

———

BURTON-UPON-TRENT:
WHITEHURST, HIGH-ST.
LONDON:
J. AND C. MOZLEY, 6, PATERNOSTER-ROW.
———
1857.

The frontispiece of Paul Richardson's 1857 volume of poems. Robert Ratcliff, who wrote his name on this copy, was a director of Bass'. At one time he resided at one of Bass' town houses, 65 High Street, but he was principally active in developing the family's estate at Newton Solney. Robert and Richard Ratcliff built the Corporation Baths, presenting them to the town in 1875, and the family later added further improvements.

Burton No. 1 Branch.

Corporal W. HARRISON,
1/6th North Staffs. (T.F.)   *Killed in Action.*

These heroes are dead. They died for us. They are at rest. They sleep . . . . . . under the solemn pines, the sad hemlocks, the tearful willows, and the embracing vines. They sleep beneath the shadows of the clouds, careless alike of sunshine, or of storm, each in the windowless palace of Rest. Earth may run red with other wars —they are at peace. In the midst of battle, in the roar of conflict, they found the serenity of death. I have one sentiment for soldiers, living and dead: cheers for the living: tears for the dead.
Col. R. G. Ingersoll.

The sentiments expressed in the quotation from 'Our Braves' by Paul Richardson were to be echoed many times in years to come. It is interesting to compare them with the words quoted for this series of First World War portraits issued by the Workers' Union to commemorate fallen comrades. Corporal Harrison was one of many Territorial Force volunteers to join the 1/6th North Staffs Regiment and to die in action. Denis Stuart's *County Borough History* (Part One) contains a full account of the Union, which included many brewery workers. The Union was founded in 1893, with the Burton branch being established in 1909 and the Swadlincote branch in 1907.

A photograph by Richard Keene showing Burton's old town hall, where Paul Richardson read his works in 1862, although probably not taken until shortly before demolition in 1883. Three pubs feature prominently: The Man In The Moon on the left, the Royal Oak before alterations and the Elephant and Castle. The distant chimney belongs to Evershed's brewery off Bank Square. Alongside Andressey Bridge is the stone from above the central window, recording the hall as a gift from the Earl of Uxbridge in 1772. The posters advertise a rabbit show, admission twopence.

Richard Keene was a pioneer Derby photographer from the early 1860s. His Derby studios were in Irongate. The Burton studio appears here, displaying its 1878 date of establishment, and it produced many high quality Burton area photographs and postcards. Keene also operated a servants' registry office at 52 High Street, an old property which, by 1911, had become Warr's the newsagents and tobacconists, a business which remained here for some sixty years. This building still stands.

Paul Richardson would have been familiar with this scene. In 1863 John Burton & Sons established a photographic studio over the High Street shop of H. Steer, the jeweller. Burton's signboard appears on the left with examples of portraits and local views in and below Steer's window. Hallam's shop was established in 1768. As well as being general druggists they advertised their horse powders and cow drinks but dressing their old style, shuttered window was hardly a strong point. Rebuilding saw Hallam's moving to No. 22 and this site is now Lancaster and Thorpe, and Briggs' shoe shop.

This print shows the town that Paul Richardson knew while also recording the brief period when both the ancient and the new Burton bridges stood together. John Richardson, Paul's uncle, laid the first stone of the new bridge on 23 February 1863. It was opened with great ceremony by the Marquis of Anglesey on 22 June 1864. The inevitable luncheon and speeches followed with John Richardson, as High Bailiff, occupying the chair. The subsequent removal of the old bridge, which was at least twelfth century, deprived Burton of a noted ancient monument and potential tourist attraction.

58

Eight
Patterns of Change

Because this book is concerned with recording the past, it is inevitably a story of change. This is reflected through the area's buildings, transport, fashion, customs, popular taste, provision of utilities, social attitudes and so forth. Here we look briefly at the pattern of some of those changes and the consequent impact on present day scenes.

This print from 1847 looks over Stapenhill towards Burton from the top of the hill on Stanton Road. The still rural village, with just 10 farms, had fewer than 600 inhabitants who mainly lived near the church and the ferry. Burton, with its small adjoining villages Branston, Horninglow, Stretton, Stapenhill and Winshill, had a total population of around 9,000. This figure practically doubled over the next decade as the town's industries, especially brewing, expanded. With that development and improved communications, commerce and housing moved ever outwards to incorporate the old villages within the growing town.

Thatched properties were scarce in Burton but one example was the old farmhouse on the corner of Woods Lane and Stanton Road. This photograph from around 1900 shows it when Mr John Wilkinson farmed there and also operated the horse buses from Stapenhill Green to the station. Their scheduled time was eighteen minutes and they left every half-hour each way, from 8.40 a.m. to 9.00 p.m. The house was subsequently rebuilt and the farm worked by Mr A.J. Evans. Cows were still brought in for milking until after the Second World War, but the farm site is now a supermarket and car park.

A case for 'The House Detectives'! These typical nineteenth-century Stapenhill cottages on Ferry Street corner are still there, although today's scene illustrates an early commercial conversion. The stepped wall and splendid gas lamp disappeared in the early 1900s when the Burton Co-op built their Main Street branch premises. But look above the present day shops and see how the two properties on the left were incorporated into the rear of the Co-op building, an ingenious adaptation which has left original rear rooms and other features clearly recognizable inside.

Older parts of Winshill remained truly rural into the twentieth century. Although a gas lamp has appeared in Brough Road, these cottages depended on pumps such as the one in the centre with butts collecting rainwater, or the spring and stream in Berry Hedge Lane for their water supply. Only after the water tower on Waterloo Clump was built in 1904 did a piped water supply become efficient, but this lane remained a quiet haven for children and free-range chickens. Burton reservoir dated from 1882.

Cottages, Walton-on-Trent.

There might not always be the alternative of a spring available as there was in Winshill. Some houses depended on a well or pump for all their water, several properties often relying on the one source. This picturesque row of cottages, photographed at Walton around 1904, shows how important it was to protect the pump, seen here tightly wrapped in a straw jacket to withstand wintry weather. Next time you drive through Ticknall notice the water pumps there, no longer used, but preserved in situ along the main streets.

BLACKSMITHS CORNER, BARTON

A reminder from Barton of the days of horse traffic: the village had four blacksmiths in the early 1900s. Local inns such as the Smith's Arms, Branston, and the Horseshoe Inn, Tatenhill, recall the importance of the blacksmith in each community. In 1900, the seventeen Burton blacksmiths included a Mrs Dooley – did she wield a hammer herself? This picture looks up Utter Hill from Efflinch Lane corner where a former smithy still stands across from the ancient Three Horseshoes, where the landlord was once also the blacksmith.

Both scenes on this page were taken by the Derby photographer, F.W. Scarratt. In the early 1930s it was new council house development in Tutbury that attracted his attention and here he records early building in Park Lane, complete with typical road vehicles of the period, although the scene still retains traces of the lane's previous rural appearance.

.S. Simnett nearly foxed us here. No map, directory or old inhabitant could explain The Moat. A Barton walkabout revealed the crenellations of today's Castle House, previously known as The Grove. Built in 1730 and now three residences, this façade is hidden by housing on Holland Park estate. From 1891 census returns, Barton historian Steve Gardner then discovered that a Burton solicitor, Mr Jennings, lived here with family and servants and it was indeed called The Moat. This is a good example of a surviving house having altered its outlook, layout and title.

This picture of Main Street, Branston, illustrates another present day pattern. This house and garden stood until after the Second World War before being replaced by a row of bungalows adjoining the war memorial. Similarly, Branston Hall, opposite, stood behind red brick walls. Behind the remaining length of wall are new houses in once rural Clay's Lane, which now leads to a large housing complex. Talking to elderly Branston residents has yielded valuable information to record but not, unfortunately, the name of the family artistically grouped here round 1900.

Just as with housing for a growing population, industrial areas too had to be established away from the town centre. In 1916 the Silvertown Company acquired a new site at Horninglow. After various mergers and changes of ownership this works became BTR (British Tyre and Rubber) and in the early 1930s the factory was considerably enlarged. Here, construction work is in progress. Note the wooden scaffolding, not a tin hat in sight and the builders' cart of unusual design.

In 1929 it was Stretton's turn to have industry encroaching on fields around the village. Although situated outside the county borough boundary, Burton Corporation owned the land and was able to bring Pirelli to the town by offering favourable terms which included Corporation sewerage and electricity services. Like Horninglow, Stretton also became aware of the aromas associated with the rubber industry. This view shows the factory in its early days.

KINGS BROMLEY MANOR

There were also notable changes of a different sort altering the traditional countryside both nationally and locally. From the 1870s agricultural depression affected not only farm workers but the other end of the social scale as well. With reduced income and increasing taxation, many country estates found difficulty maintaining their position, often resulting in the demolition of the house and the break-up and disposal of the land. With the addition of death duties after 1918 and the decease of many heirs to succession in the First World War, house losses ran into hundreds. The consequences of the Second World War with requisition for military or other uses, sealed the fate of hundreds more large houses before the full realization of the disastrous loss of heritage. John Harris, an organizer of the 'Destruction of the Country House' exhibition of 1974, revealed that in 1955 alone a major country house was destroyed on average every two and a half days. King's Bromley Manor was an early casualty, demolished around 1930. An attractive Georgian mansion, it is not well documented. It was the home of the Lane family, descendants of Colonel and Jane Lane who aided the escape of Charles II from Moseley Old Hall in 1651. The Lanes moved to King's Bromley from Bentley Hall (Staffs). The Victorian water tower survived and like many former country house features was adapted for conversion into a residence.

Other local country houses lost included: Rolleston Hall, c. 1928; Drakelow, 1934; Etwall, 1950; Longcroft, 1952; Byrkley Lodge, 1953; and the old Yoxall Lodge. In the devastating year of 1955 Egginton Hall joined the list. Egginton was the home of the Every family and was rebuilt after an earlier mansion burnt down in 1736. The architect was Samuel Wyatt, one of a family of architects with local associations. He was a brother of James Wyatt and uncle of Jeffrey Wyatt who changed his name to Wyatville and was knighted by George IV for his work at Windsor Castle. Sir Jeffrey designed Bretby Hall when it was rebuilt in 1777. Egginton provides another twist in these patterns of change. As in many instances, the estate was used by the military in the First World War and huts were established in the grounds. The old days of country house life were not to resume, however, and in 1938 Egginton was taken over by the RAF and occupied until 1947. Then, like other cases where a hutted camp had grown up around a house, Repton Rural District Council decided to ease their post-war shortage of accommodation by acquiring the huts for housing. Nearly 100 families were temporarily housed here at different times awaiting new homes, until 1954 when the council was able to dismantle the huts. The house itself had sadly deteriorated and was soon to be added to the sorry list of 1955 demolitions.

The immediate post-war years also saw intensive house building among the rolling hills above Winshill. The Manners estate (owned by the brewing family) was planned in the last days of Empire, hence Empire Road and the naming of avenues, crescents, closes and drives after cities of the Dominions, although the Empire was soon to become the Commonwealth of independent nations. The photographer surely came here on a Monday: note the lines of washing on the far right. There were no local laundrettes yet (Britain's first came in 1949) and few people had any sort of washing machine.

In the town there was increased clearance of older properties. The process began between the wars with removal of some of the old courts and rows built behind principal streets and adjoining brewery premises whose workers they had often housed. However many, like this row at the back of Guild Street, lasted into the 1970s and a few have even survived until the end of the twentieth century. In such rows complete little communities existed, tucked away and unnoticed, their only access a small entry or passageway.

Post-war roadworks included A38 widening and the Burton bypass to relieve the town centre and Branston village of congestion. Landmark losses included the Paul Pry at Alrewas where Automobile Association patrolmen sometimes controlled traffic at a dangerous crossroads and saluted AA members. A yellow motorcycle would be parked nearby with its coffin-like sidecar for tools. *Paul Pry* was the title of a play by John Poole from 1825. The inn existed in 1841 so its untraditional name may have caused misgivings similar to those over modern names like The Wasp and Rotten Apple.

About a mile from where the Paul Pry stood, the A513 Tamworth road passes under the railway. Here were steps that led up to Croxall station, originally built in 1840 as Oakley and Alrewas. When Alrewas got a new station on the Lichfield line in 1849 it was simply named Oakley after a nearby farm, before becoming Croxall in 1856. It never thrived, however, and closed in 1928.

From the 1960s many Burton streets underwent considerable change, as in this Station Street scene from outside the demolished Mayor's Arms. The signal box controlled Worthington's level crossing before it advertised petrol for the Burton Automobile Company. It is a pity that one of the town's many signal boxes was not retained as a feature. This is now the junction of Worthington Way and the car park entrance. It no longer has: street parking; Eaton's café; Leigh, fishmonger; Ada Waldron, crafts; New Inn; Maypole; Roberts and Birch; or Baxter's, butchers.

In villages, as in towns, post-war changes often altered familiar scenes and heralded the end for interesting, historic or attractive buildings. One example in Barton was Wales Lane with the 1960s development of Collinson Road. The former village workhouse, fire shed and lock-up were lost from just behind where the photographer stood. Some cottages on both the left and right disappeared, along with the Wesleyan chapel. They have been replaced by Radhurst Rise and other new properties while the old name of Penny Hill Lane has also passed out of use.

Apart from Croxall (and Branston station which closed in 1930), commuters could travel to Burton by rail until after the Second World War from Horninglow, Stretton, Rolleston, Tutbury, Barton and Walton, Elford, Alrewas, Repton and Willington, Egginton, Gresley, Woodville, Swadlincote, Moira and Ashby. Tutbury was later reopened but its direct link to Burton had gone. This photograph illustrates various patterns of change because the first railway here replaced the old Bond End canal. There were then extensions to establish Shobnall sidings and the Dallow Lane branch of the London and North Western Railway. Next, as road traffic proliferated, the rail network was constantly cut back and Burton, once a very busy rail centre with miles of additional private lines serving the breweries, was left with one main line. The tracks here were lifted in November 1967. This view looks towards the once notorious low Moor Street road bridge, but now a new road sweeps over the railway and here there are two roundabouts sending ever increasing road traffic to the A38 and a growing industrial estate. There is perhaps a certain irony about the scene as the government is proclaiming a need for more public transport and cuts in pollution and road congestion. One relic surviving from this area today is the fine Midland signal box from Shobnall Maltings, which is preserved in a private collection.

Nothing remains of the bridge on Hawkins Lane that led to euphemistically named Mount Pleasant and provided this grandstand view of the maze of railways once covering this area that is now an industrial estate. The Hay branch swung off left and wagons can just be seen on the Sanders branch. Here the LNWR water tank, coaling stage and engine shed can be seen while, to the right, the lines sweep round to their Horninglow Street goods station with its extensive sidings. There is a little greenery where Scalpcliffe tops the roof lines of Bass ale stores and Anderstaff Lane maltings.

Views of Salt's brewery are not common but Simnett has certainly gone 'behind the scenes' with this picture of Salt's brewery yard beyond the east end of High Street, near the Bargates. There are piles of wooden crates, assorted carts and a good example of a horse-drawn floater advertising Salt & Co.'s Burton Stout. Private open wagons for coal and a Midland Railway van have come in from the Hay branch. Nonchalant roof repairers watch the photographer and Burton Brewery Company's premises are just visible to the far left.

This multi-view of Bass brewery scenes symbolizes the changes involving the town's principal trade. Except for the water tower almost everything here has gone, yet today, following the takeover of Carlsberg Tetley, Bass now spreads over extended areas of the town. New buildings designed for modern brewing techniques have replaced nearly all the old traditional sites, leaving only Wolverhampton and Dudley Breweries (superseding Marstons) and the Bridge Brewery as independent brewers. Even as we go to press, there are plans for a Multiplex cinema and leisure centre on the site of Bass' famous middle yard.

Perhaps the final brewery scene for this chapter is appropriately a sad winter view of the early 1960s with dereliction already apparent among the former brewery buildings behind the east side of High Street. The railway lines have been removed and the once familiar skyline will be replaced by a shopping centre, bowling alley, leisure complex and swimming bath; new library and modern brewery offices. As is often the case, there is an apt quotation taken from Latin that really sums it all up: 'Times change and we change with them.'

Those who once toiled in potteries and mines around Swadlincote and took for granted the clay pits, collieries and spoil tips, could never have visualized a day when landscaping would remove most traces of those scenes and modern processes would banish the fumes of the old salt glazing kilns. Perhaps nothing contrasts more strikingly than to climb Hill Street today, where the 1 in 12 gradient taxed the old Ashby trams, and see the performers on the artificial ski slope created out of yesterday's industrial devastation.

One of the significant environmental changes of the twentieth century was the closure of the South Derbyshire and Leicestershire coalfields and the restoration of some of the sites to form parts of the new National Forest. Moira and Donisthorpe Collieries held an annual hospital parade and gala: this scene shows the 1914 procession. The National Forest offices are now on the Moira Colliery site and Donisthorpe site is being developed as a new country park. The float in the photograph is that of Donisthorpe Colliery Ambulance Corps.

Perhaps we can reflect on changing times by looking at the Burton Statutes Fair of 1890, when it was still the annual hiring fair for agricultural servants. It was reported, however, that there seemed to be a falling off in numbers of those seeking employment compared with previous years. There was no mention either of the old custom of wearing a coloured ribbon to signify the type of job being sought when touting the pubs around the Market Place area. When a labour exchange was opened after 1905 the Statutes soon became entirely a pleasure fair and it appears that past customs were already in decline. Nevertheless, an account of the day still reads rather like a livestock market report: 'Men were somewhat scarce but experienced cowmen obtained £14 to £15.50; less experienced men and strong youths, up to £9.50; while lads, the most numerous, were picked up at from £6 to £8.' These were live-in, all-found wages per year as against an average agricultural weekly wage at this time of around 90p a week. For 1890 an innovation was the hiring of female servants at the Shaftesbury Institute, 206 Station Street, instead of at the fair itself. Even refreshments were provided 'at moderate charges'. 'Young girls commanded up to about £6.50; women fit for trustworthy positions up to £15.' On being hired, the contract used to be sealed by the new master handing over a shilling. This would probably be spent at the fair where simple amusements like shooting galleries, merry-go-rounds and 'three throws a penny' were reported as doing brisk business. The booth in front of the parish church housed boxing and wrestling. The Shaftesbury Institute was named after the great philanthropist, the 7th Earl of Shaftesbury who had been active in many aspects of social welfare and reform. Around 1896 the YWCA was established at a new Shaftesbury House on the New Street and Orchard Street corner where an ornamental inscription still remains on the decorative brickwork.

Nine

A Man Who Liked Reading

Shortly before Christmas 1946 Mr Herbert F. Hughes retired after thirty-four years service with Messrs S. Briggs & Co. Ltd, the Burton engineering firm. There was a presentation ceremony which seems to have been a private occasion – at least no account or photograph can be found in the local press.

Fifty years later, however, a chance discovery led to this presentation being brought to light. In an Isle of Wight bookshop I spotted a copy of Charles Underhill's History of Burton upon Trent. It is always worth looking inside a book even if you already have a copy and, because of what had been added on the flyleaves at the front and back, this Isle of Wight copy conjured up aspects of the local scene as the halfway point of the twentieth century approached.

From his colleagues and friends, Mr Hughes was presented with a cheque, a copy of Underhill's history and twenty-four other volumes. After the inscription recording this there are forty-six signatures against which, by means of a number code, Mr Hughes (one assumes) has recorded where each of them was employed within the firm: a roll-call of the Briggs' company at that time. On the rear blank leaf he further listed the title and author of the two dozen other books which must have ensured plenty of good reading during his retirement. In addition, this offers a record of books that were popular and in print at that date. Many of them have stood the test of time and are still read and enjoyed today. Mr Hughes may have been asked to make a personal choice but either way it is a splendid list of books that people were reading around Christmas 1946, some of them new titles destined to become classics.

The full list was: North West Passage, by Kenneth Roberts; South Riding, Winifred Holtby; The Cathedral, Hugh Walpole; Regency, D.L. Murray; Bernadette, Franz Werfel; The House in Lordship Lane, A.E.W. Mason; Valley of Decision, Monica Davenport; Grand Canary, A.J. Cronin; Bright Day, J.B. Priestley; Life Line, Phyllis Bottome; Memory Hold The Door, John Buchan; Reluctant Widow, Georgette Heyer; Prisoner of Zenda, Anthony Hope; Eight Oaks, Stephen Lister; Then and Now, Somerset Maugham; Pageant of the Years, Phillip Gibbs; That Lady, Kate O'Brien; Trevelyan's English Social History; George Bernard Shaw at 90; For Whom The Bell Tolls, Ernest Hemingway; The Razor's Edge, Somerset Maugham; and three works by Joseph Conrad, The Shadow Line, The Secret Agent and Romance.

Although the war was over there was no way that Christmas 1946 could represent a return to the old pre-war Christmases. There was still rationing of basic items and in some respects the situation had worsened. Bread had been rationed for the first time ever during the summer while the fat ration was reduced from 8oz a week to 7oz, sugar to 8oz, jam or honey 4oz, liquid milk around 2 pints a week, cheese 3oz and coffee to 2oz. Meat rationing was fixed by price, at one stage a shilling's worth per person with a real egg every fortnight. Utility clothing on coupons and furniture did little to raise spirits. Neither did such suggestions as a Ministry of Food recipe for squirrel pie.

The Brewers' Society issued a Christmas notice locally about wines and spirits. Although there were supplies at fixed prices, there was not enough to go round and it was hoped that the public would not blame wine merchants and would exercise restraint. Typical prices were sherry 15s 6d, rum 27s and champagne 37s.

Many members of the armed forces were, of course, not yet home again and conscription was still in force. At least some of those serving overseas missed the fierce winter which struck immediately after Christmas. A heavy January 1947 snowfall was followed by a severe frost with the lowest temperature recording of 28 degrees of frost. This lasted until mid-March. Even after that further snow fell until final thawing in early April led to serious flooding. With shortages of coal and petrol, keeping warm was a problem and transport was also badly affected. With no television to watch, people often found the radio and a good book the best ways of relaxing during this drab period. At least it was followed by a truly magnificent summer.

As a footnote, how about this 'very acceptable' alternative to rich Christmas pudding, which was given publicity at this time?

'War and Peace Pudding: Mix together one cupful of flour, one of breadcrumbs, half a cupful of suet and half a cupful of mixed dried fruit. Add a cupful of grated raw potato, a cupful of grated raw carrot and a level teaspoonful of bicarbonate of soda dissolved in two tablespoonfuls of hot water. Mix all together, turn into a well-greased pudding bowl and boil or steam for at least 2 hours.'

In another publication of the period there were 200 carrot recipes to choose from. I was told of one Burtonian who took a mouthful of carrot marmalade and promptly went outside to throw the lot onto the compost heap.

Quite apart from shortages and 'making do' as Britain slowly recovered from the war years, it is fascinating to consider just how many things we did not have in 1950 when the popular magazine Picture Post published its special edition reflecting 'The Half Century'. To name but a few there were no convenience foods, flavoured crisps, tea bags, cheque cards, plastic carrier bags, felt-tip pens, tights, bar codes, postcodes, self-service petrol stations, driver-only buses, MOT tests, car safety belts and no VAT. Many readers will be able to add to what the second half-century has brought us: both good and bad.

Anyway, let us hope that Mr Hughes enjoyed a good read. A similar presentation today would no doubt see the conventional cheque accompanied by a portable television set rather than books.

Most of the old Union Street has now gone, including this not unattractive building erected in 1879 by public subscription as the Burton Institution. In 1894 it was transferred to the Corporation, opening as the Free Library in 1897. It also housed a reading room, a subscription library, the School of Science and the School of Art and Craft. It remained as Burton Library until the new building of 1976 was opened. Our keen reader, Mr Hughes, was no doubt familiar with these premises and the inked pad and adjustable date stamp system of issuing books.

High Street, an unusual south-facing view. It was decorated for Queen Victoria's Diamond Jubilee in 1897. On the left are Howarth's shoe shop and the old façade of the Star Inn with a lamp recording that it was the headquarters of the Burton Bicycle Club. On the other side, with the white flagpole, is Darley's where Burton's first (subscription) library was established after W.B. Darley set up his shop and printing works in 1827. By 1838 it had 1,500 volumes. The premises were extended back but the front disguises an original building of 1586. Herratt's wool shop next door was also of early origin.

Briggs & Co., now in Derby Street, absorbed the Trent works of Robert Morton & Co. and occupied an area which previously included Morton's bowling green and Morris' nurseries, adjoining the Cattle Market and the Smithfield hotel. This is the opposite side of Derby Street from the corner of Derby Street East, which explains the enamel name plate halfway along Derby Street, around 1902. Slightly left was the Baptist Tabernacle: the minister, Revd Askew, lived at No. 80 and provided publicity for the newly opened High Street YMCA. Nos 81 to 91 are shown, with the neat railings that were removed for scrap in the 1940s.

The area now occupied by Briggs' also included the Trent Cold Storage and Ice Company and this photograph shows both staff and stock standing to attention. A big ice house like this would supply small shops without refrigeration facilities. Here too was one of several independent Burton cooperages. At the British Industries Fair of 1948 one invention was an aluminium beer barrel. Regarded as a novelty then, it eventually ended Burton's coopering trade.

Truman's Black Eagle brewery was perhaps the most prominent feature of Derby Street. Established in London in 1666, this firm came to Burton in 1873, taking over premises built by Phillips' brewery in 1860, as elaborated in publicity dated November 1877. The fine view from the railway also shows the two malthouses that adjoined on the south side, towering over Derby Street. The brewery was demolished in 1974 after Trumans left the town. Pre-grouping wagons include those of the Great Eastern, which dispatched large quantities of grain to Burton breweries, and those of Hall's Swadlincote Collieries supplying fuel.

TRUMAN, HANBURY, BUXTON & CO.
LONDON.
1 NOV. 1877.

ESTABLISHED AT BURTON ON TRENT 1873.
THE BREWERY ENLARGED & FITTED WITH ENTIRELY NEW PLANT. 1874-6.

TRUMAN, HANBURY, BUXTON & CO. HAVE NOW COMPLETED THEIR BREWERY AT BURTON ON TRENT, AND THE WHOLE OF THE NEW & EXTENSIVE PLANT IS IN FULL WORKING ORDER.

EAST INDIA PALE & STRONG BURTON ALES ARE NOW SUPPLIED FROM THE BREWERY TO ANY RAILWAY STAT'N IN ENGLAND, CARRIAGE FREE IN LARGE OR SMALL QUANTITIES.

SEASON BREWED PALE ALES FOR EXPORT & PALE & MILD ALES FOR BOTTLING FROM 1ST NOV. TO END OF MARCH.

PRICE LIST & TERMS ON APPLICATION.

A drinks account from shortly after the Second World War makes nostalgic reading today. Truman's Brewery (in full, Truman, Hanbury and Buxton) was then thriving locally and the Hanbury Arms in Sydney Street was one of their local houses. This view is from the 1930s when Bertha Orgill was licensee but it was her successor, Tom Bradley, who receipted a bill in the early 1950s. For just under £6.50 he supplied 9 gallons of bitter (£3), 7 bottles of port (£1.75), 3 of sherry (75p), 1 of whisky (83p) 6 Vimto and 4 lemonade (together 15p). Things were certainly looking up again!

At the time Mr Hughes retired, Briggs & Co., which was established around 1890, were located in Moor Street (from 1900) and in New Street, having absorbed Thornewill and Warham in 1929. They had earlier incorporated Buxton and Thornley. In the background is part of the extensive engineering works that stood where shoppers now throng the Octagon Centre. Richard Farman's photograph also records the final day of the New Street branch line and removal by a British Railways tank engine of the last wagons to plough through the undergrowth before everything in view was swept away.

Ten
Mr Booth's Happy Invention

With the new century will come anniversaries and centenaries recalling events, discoveries and inventions of the twentieth century. Some will mark the advent of everyday things which we now take for granted; some things may well pass unacknowledged for that very reason. We decided that we would have our own commemoration for one such item.

Who now can imagine housekeeping without the humble vacuum cleaner, which will achieve its centenary in the year 2001? Although not a Burton event in itself, items acquired locally provided the opportunity to share with you some fine photographs and to give you cause for reflection next time there are crumbs on the carpet.

Our commemoration will be all the more significant if you share recollections like mine (Geoffrey writing this, not young Richard) of the bad old days of spectacular spring-cleaning when a whole house could be turned upside down for two or three weeks. Carpets were taken up, dragged outside, hung on clothes lines and battered with wicker carpet beaters. There were clouds of dust and great consternation as worn patches became all too apparent under the assault: 'We shall have to turn it round so that side goes under the dresser.' There were sudden showers on seemingly benevolent sunny days when the whole set-up had to be dismantled in haste and everything bundled back inside so that a miniature mountain had to be climbed to get through the back door. When the sun came out so did the team. A variant, of course, was the snapping of a clothes line under the sheer weight and such siege conditions, thus prolonging the entire depressing operation.

It was no use retreating indoors. Here stripped rooms were being mopped and scrubbed, linoleum surrounds sticky, floorboards damp. To help rooms to dry out a coal fire roared away in the hearth while windows were flung open to let in fresh air. There was newspaper on floors to avoid 'walking the wet' and people picked their way through mounds of dust-sheeted furniture on copies of the lost daily, The News Chronicle.

Until rooms were dry and the whole operation could proceed in reverse, chaos might prevail for two or three days, with cold meals and general discomfort before hearing the welcome news: 'Well, that's this room for another year.' It was only a temporary respite though because it was followed by, 'Next week we must get on to the spare bedroom.'

This scene is the starting point for our centenary commemoration. Burton Town Hall hosts a display of Goblin products staged by the Corporation Electricity Department in the mid-1930s. Today's basic shape and style of the vacuum cleaner is well established but the interesting feature to notice here is at the back left where the foot of an unobtrusive poster is inscribed: 'The Reputation of the Originators of Vacuum Cleaning Behind Every Model.' Note also early examples of electric washing machines, one with a mangle attached.

In the brush and dustpan days of my youth we did have a small, not very effective mechanical sweeper, but it was only after we moved house in the 1930s that we had electricity and could acquire our first Hoover, sold with the slogan, 'It beats as it sweeps as it cleans.' It was an American caretaker, Murray Spangler who, in 1907, devised an electric suction sweeper to assist him in his job. William Hoover, impressed by its possibilities, acquired manufacturing rights and produced the first Hoover 'Model O' in 1908. However, the original inventor and pioneer of the vacuum cleaner was a British civil engineer, H. Cecil Booth. In 1901 he coined the name, produced his prototype model and laid the foundations for a whole new industry. For our commemoration of Mr Booth's happy invention we are indebted to a local man engaged on demolition work in the London area who chanced to spot a weather-stained album in a rubbish skip full of building debris. Rescued, the album proved to be a photographic record of the British Vacuum Cleaner company starting with this picture of Mr Booth's original cleaner, which is now preserved in the London Science Museum. His company became part of the Goblin (BVC) Limited group, hence their publicity in the Burton Town Hall photograph as 'originators of vacuum cleaning'. Apart from its initial claim to fame, this machine was proudly proclaimed as the means of cleaning the altar carpet in Westminster Abbey prior to King Edward VII's Coronation. Subsequent early models remained of similar size but a first innovation was to box them in and fix nozzles to take hoses.

Being so bulky, the next development was a machine mounted on a horse-drawn cart for the large scale cleaning of premises such as hotels and offices. It used long flexible hoses from the petrol-driven power source, fed inside through doors and windows. We have located one early local example photographed in Derby around 1906. This operation often provided sport for street idlers as a change from watching men dig holes. Things have, of course, turned full circle in that we now run a cable outside to vacuum-clean our vehicles.

By 1911-12 the cleaning van had become a motor vehicle with the driver and foreman in front and the rest of the 'cleaning team' at the rear like postillions on a state coach. The black cap with white coat and trousers was a standard uniform. Motor cleaning vans continued to operate into the 1920s. Tramping in with their hoses on a wet day a team must have brought a certain amount of soiling in with them! Staining on the early BVC London photographs is a legacy of the album's days in the rubbish skip.

84

Development for easier domestic use progressed quickly and by 1906 the British Vacuum Company was advertising portable cleaners which could be connected to any electric light fitting although, rather alarmingly, they could also be supplied with a petrol motor. Hand-driven machines cost eight guineas and electric motors sixteen to twenty guineas.

There were many houses without an electrical supply and this is a hand-driven cleaner of 1909. For their electric vacuum cleaners, BVC recommended centralized systems with tubes running behind skirting boards of main rooms, the outlets covered by brass flaps, into which connections were plugged. It was taken for granted that the operation would be undertaken by housemaids. A Burton electrician has commented that he once encountered some obsolete skirting flaps when working on an Ashby Road property. Do any such relics still survive locally?

This collection of pre-1914 BVC cleaners demonstrates how compactness was soon achieved, along with the principle of the extension hose, making possible actions such as cleaning curtains and reaching under furniture. To this sequence some local records of progress in the development and advertising of other electrical equipment are now added.

ELECTRIC HEATING.

This is electricity company postcard publicity from 1910, although few Burton homes had any electrical installation yet. Burton had just 337 consumers in 1904 (most of them commercial users) and still only 1,026 by 1914. The 1924 figure of 2,384 then rose to 14,505 by 1934, the period of extensive installation for domestic users, although nationally nearly one third of all homes were still without electricity in 1939.

Burton Corporation Electricity Department launched extensive advertising campaigns in the 1930s and this is part of another stand at a Town Hall Trade Fair during this period. The display concentrates on electric fires but calls attention to the cooking demonstrations in the ante-room. Electric cookers could be hired for five shillings per quarter with wiring and fixing up to thirty feet of cable free.

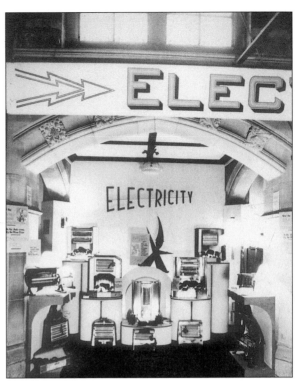

In every way Electricity can make life easier for you. For your light and to your cooking—for your heating—for your washing and your ironing. Electricity is your faithful servant and will add to the comfort and economy of your home.

On the "All-in" Tariff electricity costs only ½d. per unit and if desired all charges, including rental of cooker, can be paid through a slot meter—no quarterly bills.

CORPORATION ELECTRICITY SHOWROOMS,
BURTON UPON TRENT.   'Phone No. 2745.

Publicity in 1938 was still largely concentrated on persuading people that electricity really was the way forward for the home of the future. First local experiments with electric lighting dated from 1880 and St George's Hall, for example, had installation by 1885. The Corporation established its electricity works in Wetmore Road in 1894. From 1926 the government began construction of the National Grid to connect electricity supplies and Burton became connected in 1931. Nationalization in 1948 saw Burton made a sub-area of the East Midlands Electricity Board.

An early view inside the Corporation Electricity Works, which was built in 1893-94, but closed in October 1976. There were many changes and additions to the building and especially to the generating machinery. The tramways opening in 1903, for example, called for increased capacity. In its heyday the works used 2 million gallons of water per hour from the Trent for cooling, before returning it to the river. The building in Electric Street, which was listed in the 1900 directory with the entry 'No houses', remains in use as a trading warehouse.

The Bass hop and ale stores between Guild Street and Station Street was not only a classic example of Burton brewery architecture and building but warrants a special mention in concluding this sequence. This building became the first in the town to be lit by electricity in August 1880. It was not, however, the first use of electricity locally. On 4 March 1879 an evening football match at Shobnall was lit by two Siemen's patent dynamos. Robin Hood FC drew 2-2 with Rushall but wind affected the lighting leaving one end dark.

Eleven
Names from the Past

It is possible to compile a long list of names which were once part of everyday life in Burton and district but now belong only to the past. Some were merely of local repute but others achieved national status. Some names were very short-lived and are almost forgotten; others seemed to have had permanence and an assured future so that one took their presence for granted. This selection, by no means comprehensive, remembers some of the names that made their impact in the nineteenth and twentieth centuries before disappearing from the local scene, though some left an important legacy of original innovations, especially in engineering.

The Ryknield Motor Company of Shobnall Road built cars and commercial vehicles between 1903 and 1910, also supplying a chassis for bus bodies. *Peach's Motor Annual* from 1905 lists two 12hp, 2-cylinder models at £320/£330; a 15 hp, 3-cylinder model for £400; and two 24 hp, 4-cylinder models for £650/£700. The top range cars were comparable with models by Rolls-Royce, De Dion Bouton and Napier. Lamps and horns were not included in the prices – presumably only intrepid motorists venturing out after dark needed the 'optional extra' of lamps! This picture shows a fully equipped Ryknield model.

From 1842 Thornewill and Warham built a wide range of pumps, winding engines and assorted mining, brewery and industrial equipment. Burton breweries were among early users of the locomotives described in their catalogue but the firm's principal local memorials are the name plates on both Andressey and Ferry Bridge which they built, though the latter now lacks some of its original ornamental ironwork. Some colliery winding engines are among preserved industrial machinery.

90

E. E. BAGULEY LIMITED, BURTON-ON-TRENT
Manufacturers of Diesal and Petrol Rail Cars and Locomotives.   All guages

Road traffic now rushes along Evershed Way where the slow moving rail traffic of the Bond End branch line once ran. Houses near Uxbridge Street crossing, which still stand, appear here in the background. The tracks were used by Baguleys who, at their Uxbridge Street works, produced a range of rail cars and locomotives which were supplied to countries around the world. This official works' photograph advertises one of their standard models.

In 1916 the Navarro Aircraft Company began making components at a factory off Park Street, Burton. The photograph shows wings being packed into an end-loading railway van. In February 1917 the magazine *Flight* quoted Mr J.G. Navarro's hope that the concern would become 'one of the staple industries of the town and ... one of the leading works of its kind in the country'. It was not to be as production finished after the war. Between 1929 and 1933 the Civilian Aircraft Company designed aircraft locally: one was built at S. Briggs & Co. and flown from Bass' Meadow.

91

When Ordish & Hall closed in 1983 many Burton people felt that the town would not be the same without them, just as Swadlincote had regretted the closure of Salts. A long trading career is well illustrated in the 1909 advertisement showing founder Daniel Ordish and the little shop he established in Burton High Street in 1814 (top). There was even a garden adjoining the premises. Increasing business necessitated extensions until, in 1874, Henry Hall, former partner who became head of the firm, replaced the original property with a handsome four-storey block (left) and it was goodbye to the garden. It also provided accommodation as there were now live-in staff. In 1888 more premises were built in Station Street (right) and in 1896 these were connected to the High Street shop by an arcade, a popular feature for many years. Another new four-storey building followed in 1904/05 (bottom). The picture above is from the 1930s and shows part of the ground floor viewed from the lift which took customers to the upstairs floors. Ladies' fashionable silk stockings (and their ladder problems) are the special feature at the glass-topped display counter.

Buxton and Thornley of the Waterloo Engineering Works (1865-1912) produced a range of horizontal steam engines and pumps for the brewery industry. Their 'Burton Steam Pump' is mentioned on p. 49. They also produced ironwork, brass and copper items. This is their workforce from around 1910, shortly before the firm was absorbed by S. Briggs & Co. The accompanying picture from the same date probably portrays senior staff and management. Pollett Brothers, who mainly made abrasive products, took over the works building until the 1960s when the site became the town hall car park.

S.H. Rowley was one of the many South Derbyshire potteries mainly specializing in sanitary ware. It stood near to the former tramway bridge crossing the railway near Swadlincote station and the site is now recalled by new housing named Rowley Court. However, few if any of the latest designs for the up-to-date house of 1899, seen in Rowleys' advertisement in *The Building News*, will be around today.

The image captures a greatly changed local scene as we look from the old Midland railway bridge at Swadlincote towards Newhall. The bridge was built to take trams over the railway lines. The shafts mark 'Shoddy' pit which, like all South Derbyshire's mines, is no longer worked. The tramlines were those of the Burton and Ashby Light Railways with the right-hand line going to the depot. The quarry produced sand carried on trams for adhesion – all just a memory. Most of the background fields have now been lost to housing.

There had seemed to be prospects, unfortunately not realized, for conservation of the Bretby Art Pottery (Tooth & Co. Ltd) at Woodville. The firm's products, especially earlier works, are now much sought after. Henry Tooth, the founder, began as a theatre scenic designer and painter, extending his talents to decorative building work and art pottery. Between 1879 and 1882 he produced Linthorpe ware in Middlesborough but in 1882 he joined William Ault in Swadlincote and then established Bretby Art Pottery in 1883. The Woodville showroom, built to his own design with interior murals, should have an assured future as it is a Grade II listed building. On Burton Road, Woodville, Henry Tooth acquired a disused clay pit and built a large house with distinctive decorative features, called Tresco, which is now a hotel and restaurant. Alongside he built Hazeldene as his own residence, again including elaborate interior decorative work and joinery. This is the distinctive house shown in the photograph, subsequently demolished, and now the site of a nursing home. The interior was planned around a gallery, lit at night by a highly original gas lighting system involving flexible tubing that operated from a large spoked wheel located in an attic. Meshed grills in the hall ensured that coats and jackets hung here were always warm and dry. With full central heating as well as fires, kitchen range and laundry, it was a highly advanced house for its day. A large garden, including grotto and tennis court, could be joined to that of Tresco for public events, notably 'Living Whist'. This was a fund raising effort where suitably attired participants wore billboards to represent all the cards in a pack, and they paraded and manoeuvred accompanied by music from a brass band. At the foot of the garden was a sports pavilion and an adjoining studio used for painting scenery, display items and other art work. A special backcloth was painted for wedding receptions. Henry Tooth died in 1920 and the firm was badly hit in the following years of slump. When Henry's son died in 1931, the company was acquired by the Parker family. In spite of the adverse effects of the Second World War the firm continued to operate into the 1980s.

Burton Constructional Engineering Co. Ltd operated from 1914 on a new works site in Wetmore Lane. A subsidiary of a Sheffield firm, they specialized in design, fabrication and assembly of steel-framed structures until closure in 1979. This 1950 photograph shows productive allotments adjoining and evidence of thriving freight traffic on the railway, but a deserted main Derby road: the A38 which passed directly through the town. The background factory housed the British Tyre and Rubber Company.

Radford's Gold Medal Bread, which achieved great local popularity early in the twentieth century, was home delivered by colourful horse-drawn carts from the bakery at 86-87 Moor Street. This was Radford's head office and they had branch shops around the town. They claimed 'the most complete bread and cake bakery in the Midlands' and supplied a wide range of confectionery. Radford's were associated with catering in the town through much of the twentieth century.

While many of the scenes in this section recall larger undertakings that have disappeared from the area, there were also hundreds of small businesses which, in their day, served the public in many ways. Tealby's in Bridge Street – next to the Fox and Goose, now the Burton Brewery – were much in demand for decorating and paper hanging. Their premises housed the Bridge Street sub post office, one of three less than quarter of a mile from one another in 1907.

If you have to queue for a haircut today it will be no consolation to know that in 1911 there were thirty-six shops in town for men's hairdressing, ten of them tobacconists as well. This is Broom's Central Toilet Saloon at 56 New Street, which offered the full range of services. There is a story told, probably apocryphal but worth repeating, of a Burtonian going to one of these establishments where a notice advertised 'Haircut and Singing'. He asked for a short back and sides, and a verse and chorus of *Comrades*!

Twelve

A Craftsman Takes Stock

In 1837, the year of Queen Victorian's accession, Thomas Sanders set up as a wheelwright in Stapenhill, then still an agricultural village with a population of less than 600. The firm became well established and was to continue in the family for over 120 years, not just as wheelwrights but expanding to cover a variety of crafts and trades including those of the blacksmith, carriage builder, joiner, property repairer, and maker of ladders, gates, fences and barrows. Before the First World War William Sanders opened a cycle shop adjoining the main premises in St Peter's Street. Later the firm also became funeral directors.

Surviving account books reveal how they practised the old tradition of no job being too small to undertake and how they catered for local demand through performing a wide range of everyday jobs. At the start of the twentieth century Sanders Brothers opened a second workshop at Rolleston which tended to retain agricultural activities rather longer than Stapenhill, the latter already becoming a residential suburb of Burton. Although carriage and wagon building declined with the increase in motor traffic, the original wheelwright side of the business was still active on repair work until after the Second World War.

Towards the end of 1893 Joseph Sanders bought a little black book and carried out an inventory to record; as on 1 January 1894, 'Tools Belonging To The Shops', 'Tools Bought By The Firm' and a summary of 'Monies Received' during 1893. This is a valuable item of social history, describing all the tools and contents of a Victorian wheelwright's shop and forge. I have recorded a detailed list for the magazine Staffordshire History (volume 24, autumn 1996). Here we will omit the technicalities of rabbet planes and fillisters and look at Joseph Sanders' finances and the simple, everyday stories that lie behind his accounts.

In 1893/94 many people had a week's wage of less than twenty shillings. Mr Sanders' own wages were £69 2s 4d for 52 weeks. Wages for the various workmen he employed came to a total of £34 17s 11d. J. Warren, a blacksmith, and Lewis and Kemp, joiners, were skilled craftsmen in their own right who were called in to assist part-time when needed for particular jobs. For one such task Lewis received the quite high rate of 7½d an hour, while it is good to see Warren's hot labours rewarded in the entry: 'Welding hoops 3s, hooping same and beer 9d'. Joseph Sanders' rent for shop and yard was £14 per annum; his rates were just under £3 half yearly; and two gas bills were 3s 5d and 4s. The mind boggles at the thought of a 20p gas bill!

Equally fascinating are the monies received for the modest requirements of the Stapenhill villagers: 'Smith's barrow wheel 1s, Rodger's saw 4d, Harrison's towel rail 3d, Thompson's pony (2 shoes) 1s 3d, King's knife 6d, Dolly pegs 4d, Toon's coal peck 6d, stamps 3d, turpentine 2d, Woodward's pump 2s 3d, Mrs Bailey's slab 1s 6d, bowl welded 1d, painting letter box 6d, new hammer shaft 3d, easing Tull's door 6d, line post for curate 3s 3d, "Stranger" 9in elm plank 9d', and so forth.

At the end of 1893 Joseph Sanders had expended just under £121, including his own wages, and had received just over £117 in cash. A few outstanding payments were still due which would clear the debit balance but provide only a very modest profit. There was pride and satisfaction from good workmanship rather than much financial gain.

The Rolleston workshop accounts reflected the more rural trade, for example: Pigsty door at Spread Eagle 2s 4d, new leg Higgott's milking stool 5d, repairs to pump, washers etc. 3s 6d. The firm provided the rector, Cannon Fielden, with 143 feet of fitted garden edging boards for 17s 10d and erected a garden oak fence and gateposts with larch rails for Sir Oswald Mosley at Rolleston Hall for £7 10s 6d, inclusive of sixty-eight hours labour by four men whose joint share of the account came to £2 8s 11d. Many little jobs were carried out for Rolleston Institute and the church, chapel and schools. A County Council bill for twenty-two school hat and coat pegs, with screws, came to 4s. A 17 feet long plank was used to repair Marston Lane bridge, the bill working out at less than 1s per foot. Carriage, painting and 'picking out' a finger-post at Stretton provided a useful facility costing 11s 6d.

As wheelwrights the Sanders brothers bought, sold, restored and exchanged all types of horse-drawn vehicles, of which examples include: 'Old cart £1 15s, work and repairs £9 12s 4d, sold for £12, profit 12s 8d. Butcher's cart 10s, restoration including painting and varnishing £3 11s 3d, sold for £4 10s, profit 8s 9d.' An inventory for December 1919 showed a stock of twenty-eight assorted conveyances, total estimated value £314. On offer were a large governess cart £45; brougham £16; open float £10; two old carts for £2 10s the pair; and a hansom cab for £1 10s.

The days of 'make do and mend' have long since been replaced by a 'throw away' age or a visit to the do it yourself shop. The sounds of horses' hooves and of forge and joiners' shops have given way to the constant noise and pollution of motor transport. At the close of another century, Thomas Sanders' little black book survives as a fascinating record of a village craftsman 100 years ago.

Sanders Brothers premises at 32 St Peter's Street, Stapenhill, showing a variety of wheeled vehicles. The joinery and wheelwright's shops and the shoeing forge were to the rear and other products including gates, fencing, ladders and barrows were displayed in the showroom over the archway. This was added above the original yard entrance in 1906 and remained until comparatively recently, when it was converted to form a flat. Two members of the Sanders family appear on the photograph, which is dated 1906 and so was probably taken to record the new structure.

The cycle shop close to the Sanders' main business premises at Stapenhill opened just before the First World War. The scene is full of period detail and information. The right-hand cycle in the window was assembled by the shop using BSA fittings. The other three machines are Fleet cycles costing £11.75, £10 and £6.75. Outside is an early moped of the type that photographer Scarratt often included in his scenes. It is fitted with an acetylene lamp and a formidable bulbous hooter. Models of the time included the Minerva in versions from 2 to 3.5hp and costing £27, £29 or £32, and the Raleigh motorcycle at £25. The bath chair is built with a wicker frame and a notice in the shop advises that bassinets and mail carts (prams) can be re-tyred and repaired. In the bargain department inside there were second-hand cycles on offer from £1.50. The shop itself, after many changes of use, remains quite recognizable today at 29 St Peter's Street.

TELEPHONE 558.   COMPLIMENTS OF   ESTABLISHED 1887.

SANDERS BROS.,
Carriage Builders and General Wheelwrights,
STAPENHILL & ROLLESTON.

Rubber Tyres fixed on the premises.   All kinds of Conveyances Bought, Sold,
or Exchanged.   Fencing and Gates, Barrows and Ladders.

FORMAN. NOTTM

This curious little relic began life as a typical complimentary Christmas calendar. Some such items were often quite elaborate and were retained because of an attractive picture but this Sanders Brothers example for 1913 only held a set of six calendar cards (one month on the back of another). The November/December card still remains as backing for the little Stapenhill picture which has been inserted into the frame that held the date cards. It, too, is unusual being inscribed on the back, 'A reward for a week's perfect attendance.' Children's school reward cards were used in a few areas and were normally postcard size. This is the only example that we have come across for Burton. It seems likely that the youngster receiving it hit upon the idea of framing the picture card when the calendar had out run its usefulness.

The rural aspect of Rolleston early in the twentieth century was recorded on Burnside by Scarratt. Unusually for Scarratt this is a coloured postcard which, with its frame and fortuitous composition, has the quality of an older painting. It captures a traditional farm cart, the girls in their pinafore dresses, the flock of geese and the thatched hayricks adjoining the Spread Eagle, where Sanders repaired the pigsty door. Over many years the Robinsons were farmers here as well as being publicans. The charity almshouses were established in 1672, dated 1712 and restored in 1892. The brook today is railed off and rather overshadowed by trees.

Around 1904 Simnett ascended to the parapet of Rolleston church and took this view looking east. Brookside is to the left, Station Road in the centre and Burnside hidden by rooftops on the right. The scene reflects over 1,000 years of village history showing how Rolleston developed close to the brook, a perfect example of the comment in Rowland Parker's classic book *The Common Stream*, 'Every village … owed its original location in part at least to the proximity or availability of water.' Here the village still retains its compactness with open fields beyond and we can appreciate how Station Road was once Meadow Lane.

A daughter of the Sanders family married Albert H. Baldock of Bearwood Hill Road, another professional craftsman, well known to the local fishing fraternity. Noted for his skill in the making of high-class fishing tackle and the mounting of memorable catches, he served as secretary of the Burton Mutual Angling Association during the period 1952 to 1975. The Angling Association fished the Dove and in 1951 Mr Baldock was instrumental in launching a successful legal action against pollution, which did much to improve the purity of this famous fishing river.

In 1975 another skilled local craftsman retired, ending a long family association with traditional basket making. John Farman was a native of Norfolk where a family basket-making business had flourished for hundreds of years at North Walsham. Coming to Burton in 1953, he joined Topliss' at 11 Union Street, later taking over the business to produce all kinds of basket, wickerwork and chair caning. In the 1950s there was still brewery demand for malt skeps (grain baskets) but mechanization increasingly replaced the craftsman's products and the skills of this ancient craft.

Thirteen

Reading Between the Lines

Looking at early examples of picture postcards on p. 22 we commented on their value as pictorial records of the past. When researching local and social history it is always a bonus if there is additional information on the back of a postcard or photograph. Unfortunately there is often cause to regret that an interesting picture is of limited value because there is no information on those vital questions – who, what, when, where?

Sometimes, however, a caption may be of greater interest than the picture. For example, on Christmas Day 1911 Sid sent a postcard, showing Stapenhill Pleasure Grounds, to a friend at the London County Council Fire Station in Southwark Bridge Road, having written: 'It is raining hard here but yesterday afternoon I went for a walk by this river. It is grand and there is boating and plenty of fishing I am told. In the morning I went over a portion of the (Bass) brewery with Pa. The fire station is rather small for the number of appliances kept. They have an oil steamer and keep the gas burning night and day under it and keep a pressure of 50 lbs. The van is just like a L.C.C. van. The horses are very fine.' These are interesting little cameos of the locality and the fire precautions of the period when, incidentally, Allsopps also had their own brigade.

Even more fascinating though can be an occasional sequence of postcards which, at first sight, may appear of no great significance but which, together, can lead to the discovery of a succession of events. In between more serious research it sometimes becomes possible to recreate complete family episodes from the past. This is us relaxing and playing postcard detectives! Our starting point is the three postcards shown overleaf. They were not all acquired together or from one source but they have two things in common – they were posted in Burton in 1904 or 1905 and the name Johnson appears on each one. Enter Holmes and Watson.

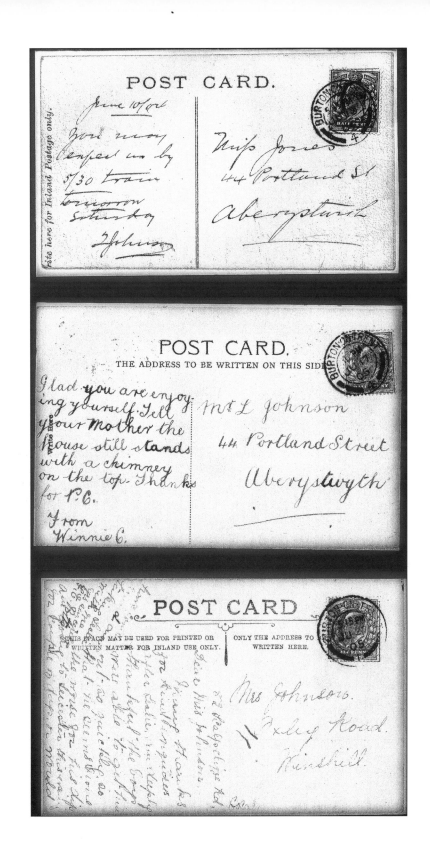

POST CARD.

June 10/04

You may
expect us by
5/30 train
tomorrow
Saturday

J Johnson

Write here for Inland Postage only.

Miss Jones
44 Portland St
Aberystwith

POST CARD.
THE ADDRESS TO BE WRITTEN ON THIS SIDE

Glad you are enjoy-
ing yourself. Tell
your Mother the
house still stands
with a chimney
on the top. Thanks
for P.C.

From
Winnie C.

Mr L Johnson

44 Portland Street

Aberystwyth

POST CARD

THIS SPACE MAY BE USED FOR PRINTED OR
WRITTEN MATTER FOR INLAND USE ONLY.

ONLY THE ADDRESS TO
BE WRITTEN HERE.

Mrs Johnson.

Ixley Road.

Kinshill.

On 10 June 1904 T. Johnson posted card number one to Mrs Jones of Aberystwyth: 'You may expect us by 5.30 train to-morrow, Saturday.' For the moment let us note that a card posted with a halfpenny stamp at 5.15 p.m. on a Friday evening could be guaranteed prompt delivery on Saturday morning. We also see that the message refers to 'us' so this looks like a family journey.

Card two was posted on 17 June but in the following year, 1905. This time it is addressed to Mr L. Johnson but the actual address is again that of Mrs Jones of Aberystwyth. It is the end of the corresponding week of 1904 and this card was posted on a Saturday so it would seem that the Johnsons booked a fortnight's family holiday, regularly staying with Mrs Jones. The message from Winnie C. says: 'Glad you are enjoying yourself. Tell your mother the house still stands with a chimney on top. Thanks for P.C.' So we now have 'mum' and L. Johnson must be her son. Winnie seems to be keeping an eye on things at home and young Johnson has sent her a card.

What do we know about Aberystwyth as a holiday resort for Burtonians? Cambrian Railways actually advertised in Burton publications extolling the attractions of the 'British Riviera' and their through carriages to the Cambrian coast in the holiday season. The North Staffordshire Railway ran a through train from Derby to Llandudno at 11.00 a.m. on Saturdays, attaching an extra coach at Uttoxeter which had started from Burton. This combined train included a through coach for Aberystwyth which was taken off at Stoke and switched to the service for the Cambrian coast. So the Johnsons could take a twopenny tram ride to Burton station and it was then a straightforward journey. Third-class return fare to Aberystwyth was 90p and first class just under £1.85.

Card three adds further pieces to our jigsaw picture. It was addressed simply to Oxley Road but another hand has added the number eleven. It is also addressed to a Mrs Johnson. The local directory informs us that the householder is Tom Johnson. He is listed as a clerk, but more importantly we have found the sender of card one. Card three was written from 82 Scalpcliffe Road by Mrs F.E. Potts and she says to Mrs Johnson: 'Many thanks for kind enquiries about Leslie. Am deeply thankful the boys were able to get Leslie out so quickly so that he seems none the worse for his dip.' It was posted on Tuesday 27 June, three days after the Johnsons would have returned from their holiday in Wales. Young Johnson and a brother or friends were obviously playing down by the river when Leslie Potts fell in and they were able to give our story a happy ending.

What about Leslie? The house at 82 Scalpcliffe Road was not built in 1900 but the Potts recently moved into a new house. Leslie's father was George Potts, a schoolmaster. This is not an epic Burton story but it is an example of 'reading between the lines' and unravelling tiny threads to reveal scenes from ordinary family life in times gone by.

The last two postcards that illustrate this section are examples where both a picture and the message combine to provide a fascinating record of unusual and vivid personal experiences.

Tutbury, four miles from Burton and also served from stations at Horninglow, Stretton and Rolleston, was a point where passengers could connect with several cross-country services to both west and east coast resorts. From 1867 the Great Northern Railway (later the LNER) also worked a service from Nottingham and Derby via Egginton Junction and Bramshall to Stafford, giving rail connection with the county town. This service was finally withdrawn in 1951. Here a Great Northern train pulls out of Tutbury for Derby.

Scalpcliffe Road had few buildings in 1890 and extended only as far as newly built-up Rose Mount Road. Rapid residential development then began during the 1890s. This photograph is from the early 1920s but there was still an undeveloped area on the right. Well-intentioned planting to make it a tree-lined avenue no doubt brought problems and very few of these trees remain today when looking from this vantage point. Some gaps in house numbering suggests original plans for more houses than were actually built and Claverhouse Road remains a cul-de-sac with no addresses.

Another Scalpcliffe Road resident, at 144, was J.S. Simnett, the Burton photographer. His family also experienced a river mishap this time, sadly, with tragic consequences. Stapenhill riverside, however, inspired some of his most artistic images, like this winter scene of the frozen Trent. The vicar of St Modwen's could almost have anticipated a caption for us when writing in his parish magazine for February 1898, 'Christmas Day came with regular Christmas weather. The fog of previous days was frozen on every twig and bough and the scene frosted over with delicate tracery glittering like silver in the morning sun.'

An engine of the Bass fire brigade about which Sid wrote to his London colleague (p. 105). The engine and crew were photographed during practice in the areas of the Klondike sidings and Shobnall maltings around 1911. This was an area with 8 miles of railway lines, sidings for 400 wagons and big stores of flammable items as well as the huge malthouses, so constant vigilance was essential.

Another Burton photographer, Ernest Abrahams, was with the Staffordshire Yeomanry in 1914 and compiled a valuable photographic record. A Burton cavalryman describes what seems to be sabotage early in the war: 'The stampedes were awful, 200 loose each night. Some galloped 22 miles to Walthamstow. I fetched 5 back from Epping Forest, 17 miles. Sent out in motors and rode back. It has almost been proved there was foul play. These were the horse lines, left – ropes were found cut, in spite of double guard second night.'

A Burtonian pioneer of the new oil industry wrote from Baku on the Caspian Sea in 1899, an early date even for local postcards. Baku was the world's first major oil field when the motor industry abandoned steam or electricity for the internal combustion engine. 'Observe the only two trees in Bacou – dead! This is an oil fountain on fire. You have only to see the ponds and rivers of petrol on the ground to understand why I grumble, especially as this raw oil is not like you get in England but treacle colour and the same thickness.'

Fourteen
Scenes from
Family Albums

In this book we have endeavoured to include a wide variety of pictures to illustrate many aspects of the local scene over the years. Perhaps no group of pictures – even where there is anonymity –comes nearer to representing the book series title of Images of England *than those which people kept in personal photograph or postcard albums as reminders of events or people deserving a place in the hall of memory. This final sequence is a small collection of such scenes, which once graced forgotten local family albums.*

This beautifully posed setting by J.S. Simnett is full of fascinating detail and can be visualized proudly displayed in a family album with the title 'Three Generations'. It is quite possible that the birth of the eldest and the death of the youngest covered much of the period we set out to portray in this volume entitled 'Looking Back'.

Though far from the sea Burton has a long association with the Royal National Lifeboat Institution. As early as 1867 the town presented a lifeboat named *The Burton On Trent*, which served at Redcar. On becoming obsolete it was returned to the town to form a centrepiece of the Annual Lifeboat Procession and Demonstration in Edwardian Days. Brewery horses pulled it through the town where money was collected and it was then launched into the Trent. In 1909 the local organization's annual outing was appropriately to Trent Lock.

Many local women in both Burton and South Derbyshire contributed to the war effort from 1939 as members of the WVS, and the organization continued to be active in many capacities after the war ended. It became the Women's Royal Voluntary Service from 1966. This wartime group was photographed at Thorntree House, which disappeared when the National Coal Board set up the Mining Research and Development Establishment at Bretby. The group is known to include Mrs Fraser, Mrs Joyce, Mrs Barker, Mrs Tilley and Mrs Earp.

This is a Primrose League picnic held at Dalebrook, the home of brewery director Francis Thompson. This political organization aimed to spread the principles of Conservatism to all classes and large meetings were usually staged on big estates such as Drakelow or Rangemore with addresses by distinguished speakers. This seems to be a smaller, local gathering for the Winshill area. With the audience almost entirely women and children, it might be regarded more as an opportunity to show off one's Sunday best and relax on a sociable afternoon outing.

No doubt this scene was cherished in later life by one of the small children attired here for Victoria Road Infants' School to celebrate Empire Day in the 1920s. This was an imperial celebration instituted on 24 May 1904, becoming Commonwealth Day after the Second World War. Inspiration for costumes of national dress from around Britain and overseas probably came from period geography books such as *The British Empire in Pictures*. Henry Biddulph of Christ Church School received this book as his Attendance Prize in 1917.

Another gathering recalls the 1911 Coronation celebrations when 13,000 school children, attending Sunday schools, were given tea before proceeding to one of five centres where entertainment followed the singing of the National Anthem. Eton Road recreation ground catered for 2,444 scholars with 226 teachers from chapels in Derby Street, Sydney Street, Victoria Street, Carlton Street, Parker Street and Horninglow Wesleyan; St Chad's and Horninglow churches; the Salvation Army; and 244 'unattached children'. Mugs and medals already presented can be seen. Competitive games continued until 8.00 p.m. prompt when 'Parents must take over charge of their children'.

As part of the 1919 peace celebrations the town's children assembled at 5.00 p.m. on Wednesday 23 July to be presented with a Peace Commemoration Medal before being fed and entertained. Many members of local society seem to have kept discreetly out of the way and given their support to a sale of work, in aid of the Girls' Rescue Association, at Ashfield House (foot of Ashby Road) then the residence of Alderman J.R. Morris. It raised £115. Black was certainly the prevailing dress colour on this formal occasion.

A wonderful assortment of dress and headgear. Hold tight to that well-worn cricket ball, it may well be the only one available. The bats too have certainly seen better days and used up many layers of tape. But there is a look of great determination about this anonymous local team with two very alert young men to keep them on their toes. You can somehow feel that their game of cricket is all-important and yearn for a glance into that scorebook to be able to recreate this long ago summer afternoon.

From cricket to another traditional English image – the maypole. Dancing is being expertly performed in this 1920s photograph by Ernest Abrahams. Dunstall has been suggested as the venue. A May festival was certainly a regular feature there in the years before the First World War and it was often photographed by Simnett. The trees look rather too verdant for May Day but it is another happy album souvenir.

This photograph captures the gentle elegance of an Edwardian garden event on a summer afternoon. The occasion is the Branston Congregational chapel garden party sale at the home of J.J. Newbold in Tatenhill on 19 July 1910. In black on the left is Eliza Shipley, wife of Thomas Shipley who was Tatenhill's grocer, postmaster and blacksmith for many years.

Although Rolleston Hall has gone, the handsome main gateway remains. It forms the background for one of the large farm wagons that were once part of the local rural scene. The well-groomed horse team, wagoner in best suit and raised sideboards in position suggest that this photograph may have been taken after disembarking one of the many Sunday school or similar parties who visited Rolleston Park for outings, perhaps coming in from Tutbury? The name Bill Appleby, suggested for the horseman, awaits confirmation.

The personalized Christmas card based on a photograph is by no means a new idea. Specially posed postcard-size photographs could be taken and printed with the back of the card already designed and inscribed with formal Christmas greetings. Police Constable Westbury of All Saints Road sent out a family group for Christmas 1907 but the previous year he had used this seasonal scene – probably showing himself lighting up – which also records The Dingle at Stapenhill as it then appeared; a stream still running down the side.

13   Servant's Hall Xmas 1911   INFIRMARY

Another splendid Edwardian period piece, this one retained as a souvenir of Mr Simnett's photographic tour of Burton Infirmary at Christmas 1911. Like all the wards the Servants' Hall has extra decorations as the staff pose with the ferns and aspidistras. At this time the infirmary was financed by investments, endowments, public and commercial donations; and by the Saturday Collection of small contributions towards provision of any hospital care.

The courtyard setting alongside a dustbin and outside the doors for the coalhouse and toilet may not be impressive, but this grand old gentleman was proud to keep this photograph of a very typical local scene. He is wearing his medals and displaying his collecting box for the Derbyshire Children's Hospital.

These members of the local Salvation Army, which was active in the town from 1886, gave much time and effort in the service of others. They include Mrs Yates. Their first band was formed soon after 1886 and, as hinted by the three generations represented here, there were organizations within the corps catering for all age groups. Only the eldest lady is in uniform and it is presumed that this photograph was taken before or after a flag day collection.

The well-known family firm Baker Brothers (Burton) Limited continues to thrive in Derby Street supplying a wide range of items for the gardener, handyman or housewife. Their family album recalls the 1930s when the business began with a travelling shop. Later there were two vehicles on the road supplying the town and a wide rural area that reached nearly to Ashbourne. War service brought this venture to an end but business resumed with the first Derby Street shop in 1945. The 1930s van advertises, 'Paints at 6d, Distemper at 4d and Gresolvent, the complete cleaner'.

This cart belonging to W.J. Roberts, a baker in King's Bromley, also supplied a rural area in Edwardian days. It stands outside the post office, run by the Roberts' family, and where groceries could also be obtained. The wall postbox is Edwardian but this type of horse-drawn cart was often still in use between the wars. In an account for bread supplied by a Burton baker in 1899, forty-four loaves cost 8s 3d and one loaf cost $2\frac{1}{2}$d.

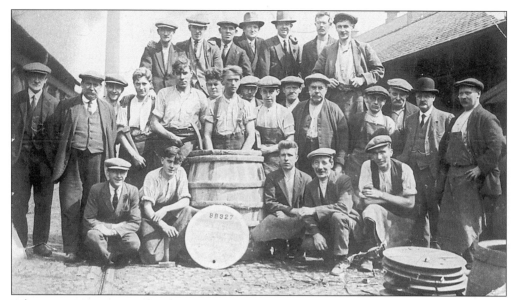

When a young man completed his five-year apprenticeship for coopering, it was invariably an occasion for a photographer to take a picture for the family album. S. Dunkerley is seen here at his traditional 'trussing-in' ceremony at Allsopp's cooperage in 1927. On completing the cask the initiate would often have shavings, and perhaps tar, poured over him and the barrel would be rolled around the cooperage with him inside. This ancient trade was to vanish from Burton within Mr Dunkerley's lifetime. Some men are in suits as work for the day customarily ceased after an initiation.

Signalman Arthur Bickley holds the large handle containing the single line tablet for a section of the Swadlincote loop line. He stands outside the Darklands Road signal box in the days of the old Midland Railway. This type of tablet made for easier exchange between signalman and train crew and gave the driver authority for possession of a single section of line, at the end of which the tablet would be handed to another signalman enabling him to clear the section for other traffic.

A postcard, retained as a souvenir, of the splendidly equipped engineering workshop established at Repton School in 1887. The workshop was an enlightened innovation by the headmaster, Dr Furneaux, to remove 'the reproach brought against … public schools of turning out so large a proportion of intellectual failures'. It was situated on Askew Hill and those boys interested paid five shillings to attend on half-holiday afternoons. It achieved a high reputation and set a standard for similar enterprises elsewhere. In 1910 the chassis for the first Morgan 'runabout' car was assembled here before going on display at the Motor Show.

These pre-war motorcycle enthusiasts were among the earliest members of the Burton LDV before it became the Home Guard and they offered not only their services but the use of their machines to form a Home Guard Dispatch Riders Section. From left to right: E.G. Cope, H. Holdcraft, F.S. Cordingley, R.F. Massey, G.E. Gilbey. Second-hand Army machines were eventually issued in September 1942 but the section had undergone intensive dispatch rider training and provided a duty rider between dusk and dawn from the summer of 1941 until the final stand down (see p. 15).

The message accompanying this photograph judges the 1927/28 Burton Grammar School Rugby XV as one of the schools' memorable sides: 'This team scored 435 points in a term – a record.' Cyril Bamford and John Rose are believed to be in the rear row. With inevitable fluctuations, the XV of 1931 was tactfully thought to be 'not quite as strong as in past years'. The school continued, however, to produce many fine players, with a period of great success in 1965 and 1966, when the First XV was unbeaten.

Burton Public Services Football Club enjoyed a successful run in the 1930s. In 1936/37 they won the Burton FA Challenge Cup. This is their 1935/36 team which recorded an equally commendable achievement of not a single foul being awarded against them all season: something hardly believable today! Left to right, back row: H. Manning (trainer), G. Toome (committee), G. Lawton, F. Holmes, G. Taylor, V. Cooper, E. Bailey, T. Birch, F. Savage (secretary). Front row: W. Frost, D. Fowers (captain), F. Savage, H. Preece, E. Boyce. This is one of a set of local photographic cigarette cards produced by the Ardath Tobacco Company.

In August 1911 the Ancient Order of Foresters held their High Court in Burton with many delegates staying in the town. A specially printed comic card showed four men snoring in one bed with the inscription 'Foresters' Visit. We Are Full Up In Burton.' Photographs show a packed town hall, the Women's Federation using St Paul's Institute. Area outings were arranged, this view showing delegates at Tutbury Castle. The card, from Gateshead, thanks Mrs Bird of the Devonshire Arms for her kindness during his visit, so he at least found good accommodation.

This faded photograph may have been proudly framed for the parlour wall rather than hidden in an album. Engine crew and shunters have posed with an early Allsopp's brewery engine. It has been identified as their No. 6, built by Hudswell Clarke and Rogers in 1876. Allsopp's old red hand trademark is included in the boiler emblem. Note the large buffers for maintaining contact when moving wagons round sharp curves, as stressed in the Thornewill and Warham publicity on p. 90.

Richard Keene was the photographer for Burton Operatic Society's 1904 production of Gilbert and Sullivan's *Utopia Limited* at the Opera House. Ina Rae and Fanny Knight played the Princesses Nekaya and Kalyba in costumes befitting daughters of the King of Utopia. It was 1985 before this piece was performed locally again but this time, sadly, there was no flamboyant Opera House for the performance as it closed in 1934. Instead, it took place in Wulfric Lower School Hall with Betty Booth and Caroline Oakley playing the two princesses.

St Paul's church was consecrated in 1874, a gift from M.T. Bass MP at a cost of £50,000. The 1974 Centenary celebrations ended with the staging of Christopher Hassall's play *Christ's Comet* in the church. Presented by Burton School of Speech and Drama, this scene recalls the late Allan Mitchell, remembered for many character portrayals in plays and at art balls. Here he played Herod with, from left to right: Gordon Keates, Trevor Poxon, Peter Clemson. The large all-male cast also included Kenneth Evans, Paul Hicken, Ronald Whetton, Michael Dukes, Terry Bailey, Michael Mear, Philip Kenny and Tom Dawn.

THE CONSERVATORY, DUNSTALL HALL

Judging by the number of salesmen, advertisements and telephone calls the end of the twentieth century has to be the era of PVC windows and conservatories. This picture shows what conservatories could have been like once upon a time. Sir Reginald Hardy's classic example at Dunstall Hall is portrayed by Scarratt but Simnett also photographed it and the sender of one of his views wrote, 'A wonderful place where you could get lost in the jungle, but the scents can be almost overpowering on hot days.'

J.S. Simnett also kept personal albums which included photographs of places visited on private holidays. The Bass trip booklet for 1908 thanks Mr Simnett for being 'at great trouble to procure views in Blackpool and neighbourhood'. One album contained unusual Blackpool views like this scarce record of the gypsy encampment with its fortune-tellers, once an attraction on South Beach before new pleasure park development drove them out. Did Mrs Athaliar Boswell, the Gipsy Queen, and gipsy Sarah, own caravans from Burton's George Orton by any chance?

Miss Jane Thornewill, Lady Burton's sister and constant companion, was a prominent figure in Edwardian society. This unique private photograph shows her (left) playing croquet with King Edward VII. The other lady is not known but the venue is believed to be Rufford Park where Lord and Lady Savile organized their house parties to coincide with the St Leger race at Doncaster. Miss Thornewill, frequently described as 'probably the best woman bridge player in England' was much in demand, often being either the King's partner or making up the four for the royal table. Society columns regularly reported her presence at Sandringham, Goodwood and other country residences where court etiquette demanded a room to be set aside for the royal bridge table, along with the custom that the players required newly minted money since the King should not handle used coinage. Stakes at the royal table were regarded as being quite high at threepence or sixpence, with perhaps an additional bet on the outcome of the rubber. Miss Thornewill was also noted for being 'one of the very few women to wear a monocle with distinction'. The dog is Caesar, the King's wire-haired terrier, which followed behind the coffin in his master's funeral procession in 1910.

A classic example of the perfect photograph to grace a family album. We end this anthology with some thoughts about this fine quality portrait by the Rock Photo Co., 45 Derby Road, a name rarely encountered on local photographs. The address was that of Charles Rock West, listed as a brewers' agents' inspector. Did he use his unusual middle name in connection with a private hobby or sideline, or was he perhaps associated with an agency for Rock's of London, pictorial stationers in Victorian times, who published *Rock's Royal Album of Burton Views* in the early 1890s?

POSTSCRIPT

Unfortunately we know nothing of those in our final family photograph, but we do know that it was taken just as the nineteenth century was ending so that they could look forward with confidence to all the exciting prospects for the twentieth century. We cannot know how these youngsters actually fared and can only regret that this family portrait, like so many, should end up anonymously in a second-hand shop. The parents' century had brought railways and steamships, gas and electricity, the telegraph and telephones, perhaps a bicycle for dad and a sewing machine for mum, and it had become possible for them to pose for their own photographic record. The children had probably not yet seen their first motor car and flight was still a dream.

Their century, however, was to become one of ever more rapid technical, mechanical and social progress, though in certain respects of some retrogression as well. What the next new century, let alone the new Millennium, may mean for those posing for today's family photographs must await the revelations of the future.

Meanwhile we would again appeal for family, local and social records to be preserved, if possible with such information as will earn the thanks of future historians.

ACKNOWLEDGEMENTS

For this book, we have again largely used our own collected material and, as always, we are indebted to those photographers, known and unknown, who have made it possible to compile our sixth anthology of Burton upon Trent and district.

We are also indebted to all who have contributed information in the course of compiling this volume. In particular we acknowledge the following for help, advice or additional source material: Mark Baker, Mrs Margaret Brenan, *Burton Daily Mail*, Burton Public Library, Don Gwinett, Tony Kelly, the late Alf Moss, Chris Pipes, Cliff Shepherd, Howard Tooth, Ben Ward, Mrs Nancy Welch and last but not least Michelle Farman for preparing our text for publication.

Burton station, as depicted in *Rock's Royal Album* of the early 1890s.